CREATIVE
NEEDLEPOINT

ROBERT CAPES

CREATIVE NEEDLEPOINT

B. T. Batsford Ltd, London

DEDICATION

To Helen, who induced me to walk this path;
to Charles, who kept me on it;
to my mother, Marjorie, who has seen me through thick and thin;
and to Verian.

First published in Australia by Penguin Books Australia Ltd 1992
First published in Great Britain in 1992 by B. T. Batsford Ltd,
4 Fitzhardinge Street, London W1H 0AH

Produced by Viking O'Neil
56 Claremont Street, South Yarra, Victoria 3141, Australia
A Division of Penguin Books Australia Ltd

Cover and text design by Karen Trump
Photography by John Brash, Fotograffiti
Illustrations by Lorraine Ellis
Typeset in Baskerville by Bookset, Melbourne
Printed and bound through Bookbuilders Limited, Hong Kong

British Library Cataloguing-in-Publication Data.
A catalogue record for this book is available
from the British Library.

ISBN 0 7134 7179 4

CONTENTS

JOAN SUTHERLAND

2nd March, 1991

Although I have been a needlepointer for over 25 years I have seldom designed any pieces, or if so, I have incorporated several figures or designs from printed Victorian or modern needlework graphs.

Robert Capes on the other hand has an incredibly imaginative flair for design and uses a great variety of stitches and yarns, creating a three dimensional effect. The subjects are often complemented by the addition of beads, crystals or pearls.

Some of his work has been exhibited recently and I am sure this book will be of great interest, particularly to those who enjoy working with the needle in this way.

Joan Sutherland, A.C., D.B.E

INTRODUCTION

*I have spent my life
amusing myself by
putting colours on canvas*

Auguste Renoir

· ·

If you can remember back far enough and recall the adrenalin charge that came from the smell of coloured pencils, pastels or crayons; or if you have ever observed a small child's face when he or she is busy colouring in a picture, filling in all the blank spaces with splashes of colour; then you will begin to taste the excitement that I have found in creative needlepoint – filling in spaces on canvas with cottons, wools, metallic threads and beads. The advantage of stitching over colouring in with paint or crayon is that it doesn't matter if you go over the lines – indeed it is often better if you do!

If you would like to rekindle these happy memories of childhood as an adult – and to share my excitement – then read on.

In these tense times many people seem to be turning to the relaxation that comes from making and doing things with their hands. Again, perhaps that interest and enthusiasm can best be observed in children, but of course the pressure of life's timetables together with the advent of modern electronic diversions have, to a large degree, sup-pressed or replaced interest in art and craft, and even reading, for relaxation. For many adults, if not most, the temptation is to leave it to others to provide their entertainment.

With this book I want to share my 'adventure' in leisure with you – an odyssey of discovery armed only with needle, threads and canvas – and to stimulate interest in the joys of creativity. I hope that it will induce you to embark on a similar quest and that you will find it as relaxing and meditative as it is productive and fun.

Ten years ago, amid a time of doom, gloom and self-pity over a crisis in my life, a close friend suggested that I try tapestry as a way to relax. Certainly she always seemed relaxed and content when she stitched away; she could even do it while watching the television! I might say in passing that what I now regard as my best pieces were all done at a time of greater stress than usual, as I tend not to work quite so frenetically at it if and when I am tension free. And I also find I *must* have a piece in front of me if I'm watching television.

This friend showed me how to do what I now know to be tent or continental stitch, sometimes also called 'half cross stitch' in the execution of a commercially printed canvas. We did not know it then, but those first tentative traditional stitches opened the door to an exciting new world of stitching and to an absorbing but rewarding passion.

Initially I persevered patiently with some printed canvases. Anyone who has worked with a needle in this way will know already two things. First, that one becomes obsessed with joining the colours and seeing the artist's picture suddenly emerge on the canvas, rich and warm in wool or cotton. Perhaps obsessed even to the extent of totally ignoring all but the most essential chores, together with the time-wasting demands of life, like sleeping and eating, so that you can 'finish the next little bit'.

The second lesson is patience. You soon learn that nothing is accomplished overnight – an inch or two of stitching a night may mean months or years to complete a piece – so tapestry enhances your psyche, for it requires patience and perseverance, while at the same time serving a meditative purpose.

Any ardent needleworker will tell you that they have sat for hours desperate to 'finish the next little bit', eventually falling exhausted into bed in the wee small hours, or have let vegetables boil dry without realising or caring. Apart from an aching back, sore neck and shoulders – not to mention crossed eyes or RSI of the fingers – you will wonder just where those hours have gone, and how it is that you have been able to forget about the pressing problem that weighed so heavily before.

While I found it both satisfying and fun to piece together the patterns before me, and exciting to watch the colours blend and the picture emerge I felt the need to create my own pictures and explore the effect or three dimensions rather than two.

My favourite needlework shop at that time displayed fancy cushions with raised-up stitches and kits with simplistic but striking designs that I was drawn to. These I wanted to try for myself. Upon enquiry I discovered that the shop held Saturday afternoon classes in stitching – and so it was that I had my first lesson in stitching, often as the only man in the class.

Those Saturday afternoon sessions proved to be my kindergarten for the learning experience it introduced me to, but it was an experience I would recommend. Sharing a discovery with others is much more exciting than doing so alone. I learned how we all approached similar subjects in a different way, how much fun it was to compare each approach and how all the individual efforts were equally valid.

Some people wanted to create tight, technically perfect blocks of colour in textured stitches; others, including myself, preferred to experiment and produce spontaneous effects by bending the rules and sacrificing precision for effect. It is this that particularly appealed to me and it is this approach that I have had such fun developing over the years.

If I wish to impart anything at all, it is to show how it can and does work to colour in the canvas and create textures; that you need not feel restricted or bound by any 'rules' to produce a technically perfect piece. If I can do it, so can you. If you have ever been intimidated by perfection in needlework, then read on because you *can* do what I have done.

I do not mean to be critical of purists, or rude about conventional stitching – it is just not for me. This book is about freedom of expression and enjoyment of creativity; about encouraging spontaneity rather than stitching a canvas of technical perfection. To work a traditional canvas in tent stitch precisely and evenly I would find a chore – no wonder medieval craftsmen worked in teams.

This is not the place, nor would I pretend to be qualified, to establish distinctions between art and craft. What I do want to stress is that you can be individual and have fun, without being tied to rules and restrictions. I invite you to experiment and throw aside inhibitions and technicalities. By all means read texts and study expert methods of achieving perfect stitches. Take classes, learn about the hundreds of different stitches there are, but be prepared to make up your own stitches if necessary, to create that special effect, and always enjoy yourself. All you need is a small amount of artistic interest and ability; and a large dose of enthusiasm. From trial and error comes practice, from practice comes confidence. Confidence leads to success.

There are those who might say that my work could be improved by taking more care with execution of line or stitch. I am the first to admit that if you look closely at any piece in this book, they are not perfect. My answer is that to emphasise drafting and consistent execution would rob the piece of its colour and spontaneity and impose restrictions on its ardour and zeal. Some critics might say that this is also a crafty way of avoiding the difficult bits – so be it. Perhaps this is one notable distinction between art and craft: the former often lacks precision in the sense that it is individual and unique. A technician may produce identical, precise replicas of photographic accuracy, but an artist does it as he sees it at that moment in time. It may not suit everybody, but it is personal and unique, and it will impress and reach others in a way that precise replicas rarely ever can.

The most important thing is not to allow the work to become a chore. Once you have become confident in the ways in which the variety of stitches can be used and adapted, there will be no picture you cannot portray; and which of the many different ways of doing so will depend only on your mood and the effect you want. Your fascination and delight in the work will extend your horizons and others will respond to your work with enthusiasm.

One of the most exciting aspects of textured stitching is its third dimension. You will find that people will want to touch it, and so they should; I always find it a great compliment to me when this occurs. For this reason I learnt early on that it was pointless to put the pieces under glass – their charm is their tactility. For the fastidious reader who wants to know how they can be kept dust free and clean, I am tempted to say 'You cannot, so do not read on!', but I can assure you that a feather duster or a light touch with the vacuum cleaner is sufficient to satisfy me.

What follows is my personal development in this fascinating and challenging hobby.

I begin with my early sampler pieces, in which basically I used commercial canvases and kits to learn and practise the main stitches, and to experiment with texture. I have tried to explain them in sufficient detail to inspire you but, bearing in mind that one can explain too much, I leave much to your sense of adventure and experiment. I share with you my stages of development frankly and critically in an effort to encourage you to persevere and develop your own skills and expertise. I illustrate how after working such a piece and with the available techniques, it is possible to create your own pictures from a blank canvas. I go on to describe some freehand portraits and depictions of subjects I have executed. In no sense is this book a text or an authoritative tome. It is to share what I have done, explain my methods and stimulate and inspire others to develop their own individuality, free of rules and recommended methods. I have tried to indicate with line diagrams and a glossary of stitches that there is little mystery behind it all.

The best way to do any piece is through a process of trial and error. I always keep a piece of blank canvas beside me as I work so that I can try out a new stitch before I put it into a design. This is also useful when you forget how to execute a stitch and need to remind yourself how it is done.

Crewel embroidery is the most common name given to decorative or textured stitching – though it should not be thought of as cruel! It is sometimes called 'canvas embroidery', but I prefer to refer to it as 'creative needlepoint' as I believe that to be more accurate and meaningful. But whether you want to call it crewel embroidery, freehand or textured stitching, canvas needlepoint, creative needlepoint, art or craft – it is compelling, great fun and within your grasp.

So go to it, good luck and enjoy the journey.

·· 1 ··

SOME EARLY PIECES:
Decorative Samplers

*He who purposes to be an author
should first be a student.*

John Dryden

....

GARDENER'S BOY

One of the nicest things about creative needlepoint is that you do not need to worry about correct tension, even stitches, or buying huge quantities of wool to avoid colour differences between dye lots. In fact you do not even need to worry about getting the colours right. It is also true to say that executing a new piece is a perfectly splendid way of using up scraps and ends of left-over threads. (Though if you are like me, you will have a basket bursting at the seams with coloured threads.)

The whole idea is to express oneself in colour and texture according to your mood and taste; your nature and eye, with the arbitrariness of the artist. Whoever saw an abundance of straight lines in nature? Of course the more practice you get with all the possible stitches, the more exciting the challenge becomes; the more stimulated and unique your own expression is, the more interesting the results. It is also true to say that each piece is an experiment for the next.

The corollary of all of this is that while you never lose the pleasure in executing a conventional tapestry in the accepted way, that sense of requiring precision is, thankfully, entirely missing from textured work. Unfortunately you still come across those infuriating experts who insist on looking immediately at the *back* of a piece to see how neat it is. If you are one of those people, my approach is not for you.

You must begin somewhere. My first tentative attempt at textured stitching is shown opposite. This Gobelin canvas was worked during those first few exciting weeks of my 'kindergarten' classes when my early enthusiasm became an obsession. Armed with a small piece of blank canvas on which to practice new stitches, I began trying to bring the gardener and his environs to life.

There is no logic in where to start a piece. Some people have a preferred routine, starting in the right-hand corner or the centre, or what have you. I have no such rule. From memory, I believe that I could not resist colouring in the centre of this picture.

Experienced needleworkers will know that when working any piece, the canvas is affected by hot hands and gets crumpled by efforts to stitch one section at the expense of another, so that the regular canvas you started with can soon become a parody of its former shape! Don't worry, this is quite normal, you have not done anything wrong and, short of using a frame to stretch the canvas, it cannot be avoided. I abandoned the idea of a frame very early on, because I find it interrupts the flow of my stitching, inhibits spontaneity and robs me of the pleasure of feeling the fabric in my hands. After all, the canvas can always be stretched back into shape by you or your framer. I took my courage into my hands early on and began stretching and blocking my own work, both to save expense and to avoid the risk of having a piece of my life stretched by a stranger! It is easy to do. See pages 111–112 of the Glossary for the method I use. Apart from any other comment I may have on the subject of frames, I find that they have an annoying habit of knocking things over or scratching furniture, as I tend to wield them upside down or thither and yon in my enthusiasm to create.

So to the gardener and his environs. By studying the numbered chart on page 5 you will be able to see for yourself the stitch that corresponds to each texture and, if you then turn to the glossary at the back of the book, you will see an explanation of how each of the stitches is effected.

I would encourage you not to make the mistake that I made with this first piece. As I was immensely proud of it, I was concerned to protect it for posterity and put it under glass. As I have said already, it is important to be able to touch the texture of your piece, so one day I will probably take a hammer to the glass! I also seem to remember that the framer insisted that it must have glass to hold it in place. I have since discovered that double or triple mounts will do that perfectly well – and add an extra dimension to the picture. You will see how effective double and triple mounts are in later pieces.

The other important principle to grasp at this stage is that this is not, in any sense, a perfect depiction. It is rather of and about me at that moment in time. Other members of my class approached it in a completely different way, as I have said. Even I would, perhaps, do it differently if I were to start it again today. Compared to my later pieces, it is more figurative; a sampler rather than a work of art.

What is also significant about tapestry pieces is that they represent a chunk of one's life, as they take so long to complete. This piece corresponds to a period when I had taken time off from the profession that I had been trained to do and was working with a friend as a gardener myself. (Well, actually, I was probably more like the gardener's assistant.) In any event, it was probably influenced by that experience and by my response to my world at that time and the subliminal beauty in it, hence the sunflowers **(17)** the grass **(9)** and the chooks **(21)**. The sunflowers were my own addition, and not terribly clever at that. Nevertheless I think they add life to the stolid though charming composition of the artist. They are not representative of any particular stitch, I would call them simply slashes of yellow stranded cotton worked from the centre outwards in a circle. The grass **(9)** was a series of split satin stitches angled ever so slightly here and there to suggest a whisper of wind from the west. The chooks **(21)** are done in the same way but I avoided any straightness of line to give them some animation and life and to make them stand out from the grass. I would have to say that, even now, the chooks are my very favourite bit!

The larger than life embroidered flowers **(18)** around the bottom are worked in buttonhole stitch with squillions of French knots in the centre. This effect is a little theatrical, but fun to do, and they act as a frame for the picture. It also prevents the piece from looking too photographic. These flowers are worked in thick-gauge wools as opposed to Persian wool or stranded cotton.

French knots will feature large in this book; a most versatile stitch that can be used to illustrate everything from stamens of flowers to sheep astrakahan or human hair, and so easy to execute.

The various stems are simply lengths of single-strand Persian wool or stranded cotton, stitched in various directions to suggest movement and depth. The lupin **(19)** is a vertical gay abandon of French knots. The large green leaves are clumsy attempts at satin stitch.

Overall the picture has been worked mostly in Persian wool on petit-point canvas. (This is Etamine or single thread canvas. See pages 113–114 for the different types of canvas.) Persian wool is a lovely soft and versatile medium, which goes further because it comes in three strands. You can, of course, stitch with all three strands to give bulky coverage or with only one strand, which will adequately cover a thin-gauge canvas. The face and exposed flesh on the gardener are worked in petit point in single strands **(12)**. Persian wool has a fluffiness that is especially suitable for portraying fabric, fur or hair. Having said that, the gardener's hair is worked in stranded cotton **(23)**. I guess it depends on the type of hair you wish to depict. This man has lank hair, parted in the middle and unwashed. His hat **(11)** has a blue and white crown of indiscriminate squares with a brim in a herringbone pattern worked by applications of slanted Gobelin stitch in alternating directions. This is an effect I repeat later in various ways, which illustrates the fun and evolution that comes from experimentation.

The scarf **(13)** has been worked in tent stitch with random loose stitches over the top. My idea, although naively expressed here, was to introduce perspective. That is, one would expect a scarf to be bulkier and stand out from the neck. This is a concept of which I was aware early on, but it required experience to grasp and develop it fully. Later pieces show some advancement in this technique.

An earnest attempt has been made to portray the texture of different fabrics in the shirt **(14)** and overall **(15)**. The former has a plaid wool effect with horizontal Gobelin stitch over two squares with intervals worked in vertical stitches. The latter has been worked entirely in dark blue tent stitch and with a looser tent stitch in a pale blue randomly alternated with it to suggest a tweedy wool. The lack of even spacing was deliberate – an early attempt to suggest the natural movement and crumple in clothing as it is worn rather than as it hangs in the wardrobe.

His clogs **(16)** are given extra dimension and perspective by being worked first in tent stitch in what I call the 'undercoat'. The topcoat is a series of straight lines or long stitch in the same colour. This gives a bulbous, bulky effect that lends reality to his feet that, rather like the scarf, one would expect to be prominent.

For an explanation of the stitches used, the numbers on the diagram relate to the bold numbers in the text.

The rake **(22)** is worked in Gobelin stitch to cover the surface. I would not repeat the pale pink stitches in the arms that inappropriately draw attention to the creases and borders of flesh. I developed techniques for achieving the effect that I wanted later.

The textures of the background are also rather naive and experimental but, even after all these years, I think quite pleasing to the eye. The sky **(1)** with its sweeping curves might just as well have been convex as concave. It is worked in a standard bargello effect. They suggest movement, perhaps a swirly, windy summers day. The flatness at the top of the curves is a mistake I would not repeat. By increasing the length of the vertical lines from six to eight or nine canvas holes, the effect would have been more circular.

The green hill **(3)** is somewhat unimaginative on account of my lack of technical ability then. It is actually a series of vertical lines stitched over seven holes, with the intervals stitched over; inventive, since by not stitching them over the effect is quite different. The large mountain **(2)** behind the houses has been worked alternately in brick stitch and tent stitch. Similarly, the buildings **(25)** are made up of straight lines and tent stitch. No further comment is needed, having finished this book, you will be able to improve on that effect.

The field of corn **(5)** is a series of long stitches over random squares, interspersed with a horizontal stitch or two; catching the vertical threads across the centre and pulling them in ever so slightly to suggest tied bundles. (This is a variation on sheaf stitch.)

The trees again are rather naive and reflect my inexperience. The central one has been worked in cross stitch **(7)** with the horizontal and vertical joins being stitched over in a darker colour. Distance lends enchantment. The left hand one **(6)** is made up of random long stitch with uneven loose stitches here and there worked in squares in orange cotton. The right hand tree **(8)** is a variation of a bargello pattern over five holes. The trunks are random tent stitch over two or three holes worked in opposite directions.

The border **(24)** was worked in long stitch over five squares; a row of tent stitch; a row of Smyrna cross stitch over three squares; followed by another row of tent stitch in a darker colour, with the same long stitch effect repeated on the outside. The flowers **(18)** peeping out over the edge of the inner border add to the theatrical dimension and suggest reality. As I said at the beginning, one must begin somewhere!

GIRL IN THE GARDEN

The companion piece to the little gardener was not precisely next chronologically, but they bear an interesting comparison at this stage. The gardener's visitor pictured on page 8 was worked for the friend who stimulated my interest in needle and thread and who shares the dedication of this book. This piece was a gift for a significant birthday.

Overall, upon perusal of the piece, I note an irony in the current context: there is a tightness and precision in some sections of this piece that the first piece lacked.

This is largely due to the medium that I worked in: this picture is mostly stitched in stranded cotton. You will find that coverage in cotton is less fussy and more distinct. There is a sheen and hardness of line that wool, especially Persian wool, lacks. Each has its advantages. Cotton is actually harder to work with since each of the six strands (or however many you choose, to use) must be kept intact and in tow. Such concern automatically affects tension, in the needle and in the author!

The precision that is, therefore, introduced has affected mainly the sky, the hills, the butterfly, the trees, the wheat and the grass.

The sky **(1)** has been worked in the same bargello effect as its companion piece. While it suggests the movement of air on a summers day, the effect is harsher and crisper than the gardener's sky. If you look very closely you will also see that the coverage is not as good and that you can make out the canvas in places. This is simply a beginner's error. I do not think that it matters too much but the perfectionist would suggest adding or subtracting strands, depending on the gauge of the cotton, to ensure adequate coverage. Here I should probably have added an extra three strands to the six strands of cotton I used.

While it is confession time, if you look *very, very,* closely you will actually see a part of the canvas not covered at all! It is too late to worry about this now, but that is a mistake that can be avoided by careful examination of a piece before it goes to the framer. Certainly the problem of distortion of the canvas as you stitch it is frequently the cause of such mishaps. Once it comes back from the framer it is too late. You need to develop a philosophy of acceptance sometimes: perfection is the aim, but all is not lost if it is dinted occasionally.

The butterfly **(2)** is worked in tent stitch for the wings and satin stitch for the body or stem.

The major hill **(3)** has been worked in brick stitch as in the previous piece but in a vertical rather than horizontal plane; with intervals **(4)** in cream tent stitch. Experimentation proceeds.

The trees **(5) (6) (7)** are worked from left to right in Persian wool for a daring and effective departure from cotton in loose French knots, random long stitch and my first attempt at leaf stitch respectively.

The lower hill **(8)** is a variation of brick stitch but this time worked horizontally and in wool for a textural contrast.

The wheat husks **(9)** are done as previously described for the Gardener's Boy piece but, as one can see, do take on quite a different tight look when compared to the woollen ones in the gardener's field.

My repertoire is beginning to strain at the edges in the red **(10)** and brown ridges **(11)**, which are both worked in encroaching Gobelin stitch, with the red being worked in cotton and the brown in wool, but they are still effective, I think.

The chooks' grassy patch **(12)** was a novel attempt to be different and the original idea behind it escapes me, but certainly it encourages you to stretch your imagination. No doubt, with my lack of experience at the time, I racked my brain for something different that would contrast with what I had already done. Hence the grassy field with its herringbone effect achieved by repeated satin stitching on the diagonal in alternate directions. It actually suggests a furrowed field, save that one would expect such a field to be brown! Ah well, put it down to experience. In any event, the chook **(13)** looks startled and startling against the dramatic background of its grassy patch. Perhaps I should

For an explanation of the stitches used, the numbers on the diagram relate to the bold numbers in the text.

have stated that to have been my intention. In fact, this in itself illustrates what I have stated earlier: follow your hunches and something good and new will come out of it – even if it is an experiment not to be repeated!

The chook is made up a little differently to those in the first piece, as the head and legs have been worked in tent stitch in pearl cotton. Pearl cotton comes in two different thicknesses – thick and thin. It is fascinating to use and creates wonderful shiny surfaces and shadows since the thread itself is twisted. Try it. (Not all stockists have it but it is well worth shopping around to find shops that suit your needs.) The body of the chicken has been completed in Persian wool in split satin stitch as before.

The gardener's friend bursts forth in a vibrant blaze of colour that echoes the lack of subtlety of the colour scheme generally. I believe that I tried to match up the colour printed on the canvas, but you should not be afraid to tone down the colours if you prefer it, and use paler shades. I believe that I did this with the gardener.

The crown and brim of her hat (14) is worked in pearl cotton in a random straight Gobelin stitch. The brim is edged in a contrasting shade of stranded cotton repeating the sheen but with a contrast in texture.

Her hair (15) is worked in standard-gauge yellow wool from scraps in my basket. Slashes of straight lines at random across her forehead burst into wonderful curls of French knots that create a slightly tarty effect, but give an exciting, three-dimensional texture as it throws a shadow on her face, which was worked in pink scrap cotton in tent stitch.

The unevenness of the stitches on her face is a mistake I would not repeat. The lesson to be learned is that with tent stitch, especially when creating the look of flesh, one must always move in the *same* direction across the canvas. I must have been lazy or inexperienced (I do not remember which) and carried alternate rows back in the reverse direction. Even if it is such a short distance as here, one must finish the row and tie it off, starting again in the same direction until the area is completed. This is imperative to achieve evenness of texture when stitching flesh.

Her bouquet (6) is made up of pale pink flowers with brown centres worked entirely in French knots of Persian wool. You will notice how the same stitch in a different thickness yarn will give quite a different effect. The large maroon flower is made up of stranded cotton in buttonhole stitch.

The various leaves (17) are simply satin stitch over an undercoat to give them prominence.

Her sleeves (18) have been done in pearl cotton in tent stitch, but you will notice that there is an unevenness in the final result. This is because I have used the thick pearl cotton instead of the thin and the cotton was too thick to go in and out of the holes evenly. Even so, I like the bulky effect it creates; rather like the crumpled material you would expect in the sleeves of a busy girl at the end of the day.

Her skirt **(19)** illustrates a successful attempt to create an effect. I wanted to suggest a rough weave, pleated look that catches the sun from the west and shades the right-hand side. The herringbone effect was created by rows of alternating tent stitch with the stitches worked in opposite directions. The right-hand side of the frock was worked in Persian wool, while the left-hand side was executed in stranded cotton. Different media create different effects.

Her outer skirt **(20)** is in pearl cotton in encroaching Gobelin stitch across a couple of holes in the canvas. It was worked in separate rows, in alternate directions, which also gives an interesting pleated look. I continued to work on this effect, so read on.

The garden is made up much as before. I would draw your attention to two experiments that are simple, effective and yet involve *no* stitches, so to speak. The large, shocking pink flowers **(21)** are simply made up of slashes of wool worked side by side to cover the surface, while the mauve and white daisies **(22)** are added to the grass with scraps of cotton in the same way. These were my additions to the artist's depiction, as were the red French knots **(23)** and the blue delphiniums or lupins **(24)**.

The background **(25)** has been worked over in patches or rows of encroaching Gobelin stitch, but where it meets the foreground I finished it off in the same colour but in tent stitch. Do not be afraid to stop short with a particular stitch if the full length is not the effect you wish to achieve. You can always join any awkward gaps with the odd tent stitch, thereby creating an interesting interaction.

The very dark green, vertical, bush-like leaves **(26)** I added to give extra perspective. These are just random split satin stitch in scraps of thick green yarn; this is another effect I have used frequently.

The tulip **(27)** is made up of rows of Smyrna cross stitch in stranded cotton; the flowers in the foreground **(28)** are done in button-hole stitch; the leaves **(30)** are an inexperienced attempt at flat stitch. The red geraniums **(29)** are clusters of French knots and I deliberately allowed them to be looser than usual. All of these stitches began to take on a refinement as my confidence increased, as you will see in later chapters.

A CHRISTMAS CELEBRATION: Learning from a Kit

All things are artificial,
for nature is the art of God.

Thomas Browne

....

WREATH

Early in my journey, I searched every craft shop for stimulation and new challenges. In so doing, I spotted an American kit for a wreath for Christmas that came fully equipped with painted canvas, wools and instructions for its sewing. (It was called 'Tapestrations by Paternayan'.) Diagrams of the stitches with explanations as to their execution were provided. I worked patiently and with great enthusiasm to produce the wreath; it has been central to my Christmas decorations ever since, and one of the few pieces I have kept for myself. If you look at the numbered diagram on page 15 you will see that the actual number of stitches is few and yet they work to produce a special effect. Working the piece was as instructive as a class in needlework, and it was a great boon to my progress.

The wreath came with Persian wool and there were clear directions as to where and how each colour should be used. My experience with the samplers encouraged me in my efforts to get it right. I would really recommend that early in your creative adventure you should find a kit that you like and try it – it will give you enormous confidence.

One vital and satisfying lesson it taught me was how to create a realistic face. Faces are frightening, since they either look right or wrong; other parts of the body are open to interpretation, but the faces of animals and people must be at least recognisably real and accurate.

Therefore, you need to persevere with them and kits are ideal for assisting with this. Artists have painted the canvases and, by following their directions, you can actually believe that you have done it yourself once they are covered in wool – and you have.

If you look at the diagram you will note that the basic stitches that create these animals are straightforward. The little blue finch (1) I worked as recommended, and in the colours provided, in split satin stitch. The vivid red parrot (2) is in straight Gobelin stitch, broken at suggested intervals by chain stitch. Chain stitch is a very adaptable and easy stitch that recurs again and again. This was my first introduction to it, thanks to the kit, and the beginning of a whole new range of textures that I shall show you later in this book. The beautiful rabbit (3) is in split satin in the recommended shades. The cheeky possum (4) is done in the same Gobelin stitch as the parrot. The blue indeterminate bird (5) (I cannot remember what he was called) has been worked in a thicker gauge wool in split satin and encroaching Gobelin stitch as the mood struck me. The squirrel (6) (with the exception of the squiggly line in the tail and the back edge of the body) has been worked in split satin stitch as suggested; the squiggly bits were done in chain stitch.

The rest of the motifs in this wreath were worked in the following ways. The holly leaves (7) were worked in tent stitch; while the holly berries (8) were worked with a tent-stitch undercoat and covered with horizontal long stitches to make them protrude, so creating a third dimension – a few were even done in blue for an interesting contrast! The fir leaves (9) were achieved by splashes of random Gobelin stitch emanating from a branch worked in chain stitch. The pine cones (10) were done in Roumanian stitch, basically using slashes of angled long stitch that were crossed every so often with a vertical stitch to give a roughness resembling the texture of a pine cone. I seem to remember that I did not follow the suggested stitch here, maybe I could not work out the stitch from the directions! The texture displayed is effective nonetheless; boldness comes with experience. I learned later about Roumanian stitch, and thought myself clever to have gone back to first principles without realising it!

One final observation about the piece is that if you look closely, albeit very closely, you will yet again find some exposed bits of canvas.

One difficulty with combining daring splashes of colour as in the pine leaves, etc. with a tent stitch background is that the background needs to go well into the other areas so as not to leave exposed any canvas. Inexperience and impatience led me to hurry past thoroughness. Still, once I had this piece made up into a wreath, backed with felt and trimmed with dressing-gown cord, I was very proud indeed – proud enough to initial and date it, a little touch that I have found very useful when writing this book! The wreath inspired me to create my own Christmas pieces, which come next. It has adorned my mantlepiece every Christmas since 1983. This piece and the Christmas stocking illustrated on page 16 were 'professionally' made up and backed. You might be able to sew up your own pieces into completed 'objects d'art'; I cannot sew a stitch.

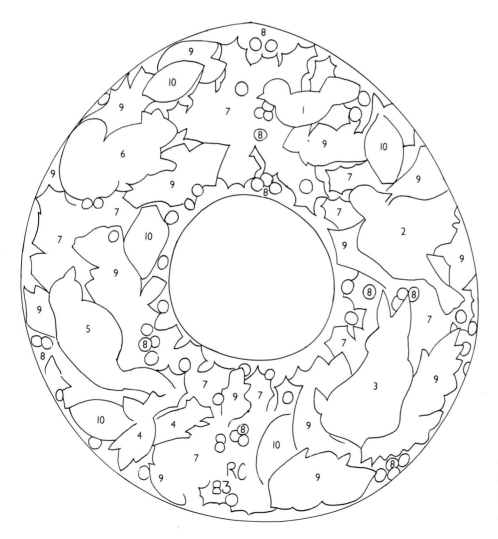

For an explanation of the stitches used, the numbers on the diagram relate to the bold numbers in the text.

CHRISTMAS STOCKING

Out of the marvellous kit for the wreath came my first brave effort at self-expression: a Christmas stocking.

I purchased a large piece of petit-point canvas and sketched out the shape on to a manageable rectangular piece thereof (the finished stocking is about 43 cm long and 25 cm wide at the base, narrowing to 18 or 19 cm at the top) ensuring that there was plenty of free canvas between the design and the outer edge of the canvas.

I drew inspiration from old Christmas cards for the Father Christmas, the bells and the tree. It is not very difficult to see whence came inspiration for the holly and fir leaves! The stitches and effects gained from my brief experience to date then evolved as follows.

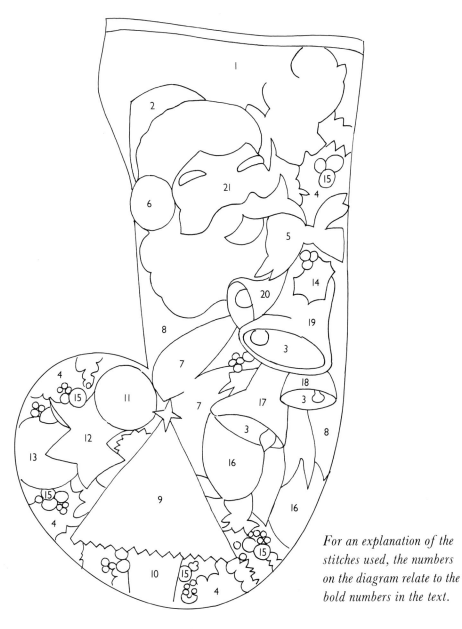

For an explanation of the stitches used, the numbers on the diagram relate to the bold numbers in the text.

The sky **(1)** was worked in a basic bargello by threading the eye of a larger than usual needle with a strand of metallic thread as well as a pale blue Persian wool and simply letting it land as it falls. One stitch will hide the metallic thread; the next two may show it, and so on; the overall effect is pleasing and uncontrived without any special effort to create patterns. While on the subject of needles, I actually enjoy working with larger needles, so often I buy a packet of different sized needles as I break them regularly. I believe in making needles suit my comfort rather than vainly trying to do everything with the smallest possible needle. One is supposed to enjoy the journey, remember?

Santa's hat **(2)**, his face, the inside of the bells **(3)** and the green holly leaves **(4)** have all been worked in tent stitch. Santa's fur, beard and moustache, and the yellow ribboned bow **(5)** have been worked in Persian wool in split satin stitch, which, as you can see, is a very effective way of suggesting texture. What is especially interesting is that it is possible to create a variety of textures with the *same* stitch, either by making it looser or tighter or by using a different thread to execute it. Here the beard and hairy bits have been allowed to wander loose; while the velvet or material look of the ribbon comes from a tighter application with the intervals between the applications of each stitch much smaller. His hair peeping out from beneath the cap is done in the same stitch but in stranded cotton, providing a sheen and coarser texture for contrast since the colour had to be consistent.

The pom-pom **(6)** is my own invention. I use this effect often from here on, it is simply achieved by threading the needle with one strand of Persian wool or other thread and applying the needle at random in and out of the canvas, drawing it firmly but lightly enough to allow the thread to protrude on the right side and not pulling it all the way through the hole of the canvas. The thread is then caught at the back as one repeats the process over and over again. As each individual stitch is made, it is secured but, just to make absolutely sure that it does not all unravel, I knot it when it is completed. It all sounds complicated – it is not. Get out your piece of blank canvas now and try it. I find that it is highly effective to produce a looser look than French knots for this sort of furry subject.

The gongs on each bell have been undercoated in tent stitch and then overstitched in satin stitch to make them protrude. The pine leaves **(7)** are a direct copy from that fabulous Christmas kit. Slashes of single-stranded multi-coloured green Persian wool with the occasional scrap of stranded cotton are interspersed here and there with some marvellous green metallic thread that I got from a favourite shop. The brown stems are worked in chain stitch in a standard-gauge wool. The red background **(8)** was intended to balance the colour scheme and suggest Santa's suit. The surface has been worked in red metallic thread in tent stitch and then randomly interspersed with French knots. Metallic thread used in this way is really very effective, but somewhat frustrating to apply, as it teases out and breaks easily. The lesson I learned from this exercise is that your needle should be threaded with relatively short threads of approximately 20 to 25 cm (8 to 10 in) and no more. This is particularly so with metallic thread as it twists, knots and frays causing wastage of material and temper! However, with all threads for canvas work, if knots and twisting occur, the threads being used are too long. A tip that ought to be mentioned here is that whatever the length of your thread, every so often as you stitch, allow the needle to fall and hang free on the thread. It will usually spin until it straightens out. This avoids knots and tangles in your stitching and allows a second wind of enthusiasm in the needleworker.

The Christmas tree **(9)** has been worked in leaf stitch with the same duplication of yarn as described above for the sky. This time I used one thread of Persian wool in green combined with a silver thread. The candy sticks are worked at random in thick-gauge wool scraps from the basket with the occasional French knot of left-over red metallic thread. The yellow tub **(10)** is made up of two rows of French knots, on the upper and lower edges of the rim, between which is vertical long stitch; below this is horizontal long stitch across the base of the tub. An abundance of silver thread in the basket allowed for extra embellishment. A word of caution, perhaps, needs to be sounded as to the importance of restraint in decorative touches, so as not to spoil or overdo the finished effect. There is still much evidence of lack of repertoire.

The large bauble **(11)** is in pale blue Persian wool in an undercoat of random long stitch worked in no particular direction or pattern, but simply to cover the surface. When an undercoat is required I soon discovered that to painstakingly cover the surface in tent stitch is a waste of time and wool. Since it is going to be covered anyway, it really does not matter how the under surface is covered. Random coverage will do just as well. The top coat is an experimental application of chain stitch with the chains joined both vertically and horizontally. This is an effect I used again later to great effect to create lace and decorative fabric. At this stage it was an experiment, but effective enough, I think.

The silver star **(12)** was worked in tent stitch with silver metallic thread. The surface is rather uneven, since the teasing and fluffiness of metallic thread I have already referred to caused me to lose patience with evenness. In the long run I do not think it was a defect but, rather, an advantage! The finished effect speaks for itself.

The pink bauble **(13)** was worked in tent stitch in pink pearl thread and then pink metallic-thread French knots were applied.

The holly leaves **(4)** are roughly sketched and worked in contrasting shades of green scraps from the overcrowded basket of threads in tent stitch. I have attempted a bold experiment into the third dimension here by re-working a few holly leaves **(14)** with long stitch persian overcoat.

The holly berries **(15)** have been worked first in tent stitch (actually if you look at the berry closest to Santa's face, right at the top of the piece you will see that I have missed one!) and then stitched over the top in horizontal long stitch. In some cases I have circled the berries in silver with random stitches. This is almost overdone!

The pine cones **(16)** have been worked in varying shades of brown from my basket in Roumanian stitch. The effect is similar to the pine cones in the Christmas wreath, and the stitch I learned from that kit. Its roughness suggests that, at this stage, I still did not know how to accurately work this stitch (let alone its name!).

The pink bell **(17)** is worked in French knots in multifarious shades of pink with occasional silver ones. The edge of the rim and a waist-line is created in tacking stitch and random tent stitch respectively. There is an attempt to create an appearance of shadow inside the bell with grey and pink tent stitch – artistic licence perhaps!

The surface of the silver bell **(18)** is worked with random slashes of split satin stitch. The metallic thread hides a multitude of sins, and the end result is effective nonetheless.

For the largest bell **(19)** I used a repeated application of satin stitch with stranded cotton, since I wanted this bell to be prominent. My imagination ran riot in the swirls of French knots in blue metallic threads; I worked them in peaks to give it bulk. This verges on the overdone – restraint came later – although at Christmas colour and glitter can be over the top and yet offend no one!

The green bell **(20)** has been filled in with thick-gauge scraps in long stitch and caught in the middle with a row of silver stitches worked over two canvas squares in long stitch.

A word about Santa's face **(21)**. As I have previously said, kits give you confidence when working a face. Certainly a cartoon-type face can be worked happily without resorting to stereotypes, especially if it is your own design. However, achieving the right light and shade to suggest reality takes practice and trial and error. One very important principle that I have discovered that works especially well for more realistic attempts at faces (as opposed to cartoons) is the need to look at the piece from a distance. Working with needle and thread usually means you are very close to the subject, but perspective and reality are achieved by distance. Therefore, every so often as I stitch I throw the piece on to the floor in front of me and study it from a distance. Such a step is both satisfying and essential. Apart from psychologically putting one in control, it is the best way of telling whether the face is working or not. My other piece of advice in this context is not to be afraid to unpick and try again until you are satisfied. With a favourite needle, a comfortable upright chair, a sharp pair of scissors and my spectacles, my unpicker rates as my greatest 'friend' when stitching. If you do not have one, then you should acquire one. Never be tempted to leave a mistake in the hope that it will improve once the whole of the piece has been worked. Unpick it and start again; you will lose that sense of panic and despair. The joy of getting it right is quite unsurpassable!

Flesh colours are tricky, and outlines even trickier. As my work progressed I tried all sorts of shading as you will see in later chapters. Sometimes, to achieve a third dimension I have found that shading is necessarily sacrificed to a degree; but with a flat surface worked in petit-point tent stitch, shading is the only way to get perspective and reality.

With Santa's face, in my naivety, I relied upon a pink line contrast for cheeks, nose and mouth. There are patches of darker shades of pink under the eyes and nostrils and in wrinkles here and there; the rest of the flesh is worked in a pale pink tent stitch. If I were to re-do this face now, I would probably try for a more gradual shading from pale to dark. Still, let us not get too complicated too quickly. One must make haste slowly.

The black rims round the eyes are perhaps the biggest mistake, since the contrast is so very sharp. I would probably choose a darker beige or grey if I were to approach the subject ten years down the track. There is, however, a major difficulty in this area since it is very difficult to match up shades of wool or cotton to get a subtle shading. Dye lots just do not come shaded gradually. I think it is quite acceptable to pick out the main features in a contrasting colour – and certainly no one could mistake where his eyes are. If you try to be too clever, nothing gets done for fear of failure.

CHRISTMAS MOTIFS

At about the time of my Christmas experimentation, enthusiasm and confidence spurred my imagination to these two little soupçon for a Christmas party my partner and I were to attend. The invitation had said to 'wear some Christmas'.

The scrap basket was raided to produce a Father Christmas who was sewn on to a pocket of an old jacket and a rosette suggestive of a Christmas wreath.

The Father Christmas was ultimately sewn on to the lid of a covered cardboard box to make a decorative container for a gift. By now you will be able to pick the stitches I used. His hat, pom-pom, jacket edge and trouser cuff are all worked in French knots of cream Persian wool. His beard is in vertical split satin stitch and the moustache a few random horizontal tacking stitches. Everything else with very few exceptions is worked in tent stitch in Persian wool, stranded cotton and metallic thread. The pale blue balloon is, of course, long stitch in stranded cotton, the lemon balloon is also long stitch, but worked in Persian wool. '1984' on the lemon balloon refers to its age – George Orwell was in fact wrong; nothing much did happen!

The rosette is a rough circle of green holly leaves in tent stitch encircled and centred with French knots to suggest snow. It is topped with a bright red bow worked in a very rough long stitch. The berries are worked over an undercoat so that they protrude and the odd red French knot gives a little extra relief from boredom. A green felt border, roughly cut, completes the effect. Ribbons were sewn on to a safety pin to secure it to a lapel – simple but effective. The possibilities are endless.

These pieces are not sophisticated, but they are fun, easy to do and effective.

·· 3 ··

AN EASTER EXPERIMENT

The artist is the only one who has normal vision.

George Bernard Shaw

....

I have always wondered where the rabbit really fits into the message of Easter, and there are many Australians who would never describe this cute little creature as anything but one of nature's pests. I guess it is all a question of perspective.

This early project – a padded box as an Easter gift for my Mother from my own design – was my first real attempt to grapple with the quandary of introducing a convincing third dimension and perspective to my work.

Introducing a third dimension is one thing, but the task of keeping the foreground prominent and the background not so prominent is in itself a mighty challenge sometimes. This is especially so since the majority of embroidery stitches are bulky and protuberant. Just working them gives a third dimension, often at the expense of the other two!

Forget about the complications of expressing the middle-ground, to ensure that the foreground protrudes further than the background is tricky and challenging enough. Where it is difficult or impossible you can always resort to that marvellous ploy 'artistic licence' – I do. I believe that imagination is more exciting than reality anyway! Even if the perspective suffered a little from naivety and enthusiasm for effect, the final result is brightly appealing, I think.

By now you will be familiar with most of the stitches I employed in this piece. I sketched the design on to Etamine canvas largely from my own imagination. Perhaps it is tempting to say that since this is a relatively small design, my imagination had a distance to travel yet. Be that as it may, I distinctly recall deriving enormous fun from its execution.

Lurex thread on the egg provides a strong contrast in texture.

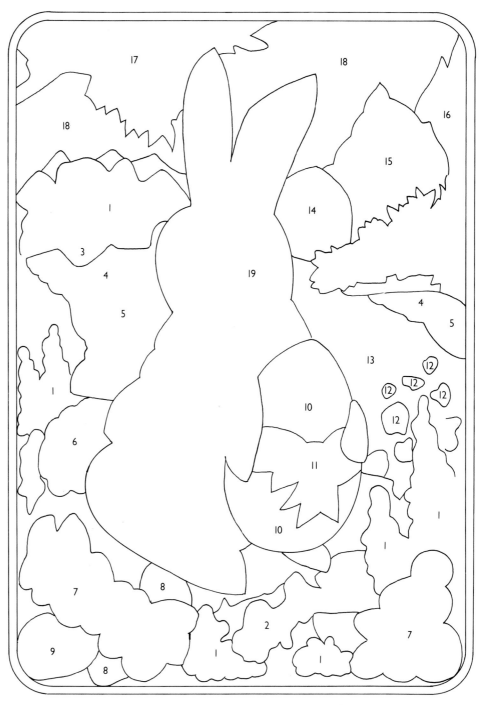

For an explanation of the stitches used, the numbers on the diagram relate to the bold numbers in the text.

The various flowers **(1)** are all applications of French knots and, with one exception **(2)**, are executed in a thick-gauge wool; **2** is done in stranded cotton. In each case the knot was allowed to remain fairly loose; that is to say, it was not an 'expert' application! I will leave it to *your* imagination to guess the names of the various flowers, except to say that I remember being quite proud of and pleased with the red geraniums in the urn. The leaves I executed in a distinctive green in tent stitch, which pushes them into the background and gives a feeling of perspective. The leaf **(3)** I gave an overcoat so as to bring it forward.

Such subtlety you might well have missed if I had not mentioned it specifically!

The edges of the urn (4) in bold, loose French knots were an ill-fated attempt to suggest gnarled concrete and certainly require some imagination to be seen as in perspective. Their redeeming feature is that they provide contrast in texture and shadows. Another time I would inset these sections into areas of tent stitch or some other less intrusive stitch.

The rabbit's tail (6) is a pom-pom executed as described on page 18 and in the Glossary. It gives an accurate third dimension to the piece, even if the tail protrudes further than the flowers in the fore-ground. It is, however, a delight to touch.

The foreground flowers (7) are worked in Gobelin stitch with the thick-gauge wool being applied in slightly different directions and consistency on each petal. This gives a lively finish to their texture; it is easy to do, easy on the eye and not really a stitch at all. My repertoire of stitches begins to enlarge through experience and imagination. You will note too that the flowers in the right hand corner have flat stamens worked in tent stitch, while those in the left hand corner have French knots; all in the cause of perspective.

The two fluffy flowers (8) were worked in buttonhole stitch with French knot centres, which I then snipped with scissors. I believe that this was the result of my attempt to unpick what had been a mistake. I liked the effect and left them. I have often used the same effect purposely since. Experiment with this idea on your piece of canvas. The lower left-hand flower (9) is the only buttonhole-stitched flower left behind!

The egg (10) that the bunny cradles in his paws was worked entirely in tent stitch with single strands of Persian wool for polka dots and gold metallic thread for the background. The coverage of the latter suffered a little since the metallic thread was very fine. A little canvas showing here and there adds its own textural interest. This is a theme I developed later, but this piece is my first deliberate use of the effect, I did not want to thicken it with a double thread or in thicker cotton since that would have interfered with the perspective: I wanted the polka dots to be prominent.

I also kept in mind the need for the red ribbon (11) to protrude further into the foreground without any competition. The ribbon is simply thick-gauge wool in straight Gobelin stitch. I pulled the thread loosely in some places, tightly in others, to suggest a tied bow. Very simple to do yet, I think, effective.

A similar use of Gobelin stitch in chunks has achieved a convinc-ing concrete look on the urn and plinth (5). The upright sections of the urns have been undercoated in tent stitch to project them forward.

The daisies (12) are threads radiating from the centre at random, rather like the sunflowers in the garden I described in the first chapter, but this time with a little more subtlety. By using several different shades and introducing occasional slashes of fine-gauge pearl cotton or stranded cotton it was possible to add shading and perspective here. The stamens are loose French knots.

The thick band of dark green **(13)** was intended to represent the sturdiness of a clipped hedge, which I think it does successfully. It was executed in Smyrna cross stitch over seven canvas holes, with a little of the white canvas showing here and there. The perspective of the middle-ground has been sacrificed for effect here.

The bushes and trees in the background **(14) (15) (16)** were an attempt at working contrasting shapes and textures to suggest depth; my lack of repertoire interferes to a degree, but it is not without some effect. For the bush **(14)** I used the wool left over from the geranium leaves to promote a balance of colours, and I worked random slashes of different lengths horizontally. A leaf stitch was used for the centre tree **(15)** and random slashes of different colours stitched vertically for the right-hand tree **(16)**. Can you guess that this is a poplar tree – an impressionist version thereof perhaps?

The sky **(18)** is in standard bargello (still, you will notice, with pointed swirls) and the branch of the overhanging tree **(17)** is a further impressionistic attempt at introducing depth and framing the picture. The branches have been worked in chain stitch in a light colour over slashes of brown here and there. The leaves are random, variegated scraps of Persian wool in Gobelin stitch – or should I say hints of Gobelin stitch.

I have left any mention of the rabbit **(19)** until last since his coat is obviously the result of lessons learned to date and discussed in the first two chapters. I have here made some attempt at shading; the entire surface is worked in Persian wool in single strands of split satin stitch. An undercoat of thick-gauge wool would have brought the figure from the middle-ground and caused him to protrude more into the fore-ground. I recall that the strictures of time, expense and patience prevented my bothering with this undercoat although, in the end, I do not believe the final effect was marred.

Far more important is to stress that you should always ensure that there is a border of at least 5 cm (2 in) around the worked section. Fraying of the canvas during stitching often reduces the surface available for the framer to work on. My lack of attention to this detail caused problems in the making up of this piece into a lidded box that my Mother proudly displays each Easter. It was only the expertise of my friend Val Landman that enabled this piece to be made up and saved it from oblivion.

·· 4 ··

A CARTOON FOR
A CHILD

Never be so brief as to become obscure.

Tryon Edwards

....

My younger son, Jeremy, was very fond of cartoon characters. At seven or eight years of age, he had myriads of favourite toys and icons. He and I both liked drawing. Sometimes we had 'making mornings', when we created things together. On one of these Sunday mornings we sat down together and planned which of his favourite characters would be featured in a design for the lid of a padded box that would be suitable for containing treasured items or, later on, for his bow ties or studs. I liked the idea that this project would be a perpetuation of our special moments together for him to keep and use in later life.

Gradually from a list of favourites we pieced together a kaleidoscope of characters that (on his strict instructions) I drew on to graph paper for correct scale and ease of reproduction on to canvas.

The picture on page 31 is only part of the whole design and completed lid that, for reasons of copyright, I have been required to abridge. Nevertheless I believe that the part depicted is sufficient to illustrate the idea, and I hope will inspire you to note the development and scope to which this exciting application of needle and thread can be put. Creating takes on extra meaning if it is for someone special and loved. I like to think that this is actually one of my most inspired pieces, as much for its subtlety as for its simplicity. It was a labour of love.

Starting from the bottom left of the design I have depicted Jeremy's teddy bear along with such special favourites as Noddy. Teddy was worked with a single strand Persian wool and a split satin stitch with very short intervals between the stitches. The seams of Teddy's back and limbs are achieved by tent stitch in the approximate spots – simple but very effective. I could have padded him for extra thickness with a thick-gauge wool undercoat, but a little boy's impatience to see it finished made me anxious not to dilly dally with such refinements! Also, the seams were integral to the design and they might not have shown up so well if they had not been given prominence. This is another example of remembering what merit there is in simplicity.

The seated figure of Noddy was worked in the following way. His hat was given an undercoat and then covered in Gobelin stitch in a thick-gauge wool; his hair was done in random stitches in a single strand of Persian wool to give it an untidy look; while his face was carefully tent stitched in a single strand of pink Persian wool of a pale hue except for his bright pink cheeks and nose. The eyes, chin and mouth have been outlined with a single strand of black Persian wool in tacking stitch. Had I tried to follow the purists' rules of tent stitches all in the same direction and of acceptable canvas application, Noddy's face would not have happened!

Noddy's scarf was loosely worked in Persian wool and his red shirt in stranded cotton in split satin stitch in different directions for the sleeves and for the body so as to create some contrast. His pale blue shorts consist of a patient application of Persian wool; they are lined in dark blue. The little pink legs peeping out of the shorts are worked in tent stitch again in a single strand of Persian wool. His red boots with their beige soles are in thick-gauge and single-strand Persian wool respectively.

Note the cartoon nature of his hands and the bent flower he clutches in his left hand. Bold dramatic strokes create an air of reality with simplicity if not accuracy. Resist the temptation to be too clever. If a standard stitch is not appropriate, go back to basics and keep it simple. The bows on his red boots are random stitches of navy blue pearl cotton in a clockwise direction to fill in the space of the laces. From one extreme to the other: the bell on his hat I undercoated in a neutral coloured, thick-gauge wool and applied metallic gold thread over the top.

Felix the Cat was worked in single strands of black Persian wool in split satin stitch, save for his nose and eyes, which are in Gobelin stitch, the former with an undercoat to give the nose perspective. His little bow tie has been worked in horizontal and vertical strokes of single strand red Persian wool and embellished with loose, random, tent stitches in single strand Persian wool in white.

For the Smurf's prominent corner I followed my own counsel as to the effectiveness of simplicity. This both assisted with the perspective and contrasted well with the rest of the piece. I worked his face and hat entirely in tent stitch, save for the outline, which was worked in tacking stitch yet again, taking no notice at all of the canvas holes or the conventional requirements.

Humpty Dumpty, resplendently astride his grey wall, beams out from a face worked in single strand Persian wool in white and his smiling visage has tacking stitch for the outline. His stand-up wing

collar is in gold metallic thread in a loose chain stitch, bordered at intervals with tacking stitches in stranded cotton. A row of Gobelin stitch in beige stranded cotton bordered in green culminates in a green stranded-cotton bow tie.

His jacket is worked in tent stitch with a gold metallic thread and his cuff consists of one or two chain stitches. The trousers were worked in yellow thick-gauge pearl cotton that, given that petit-point canvas has been used, created its own protrusion. The horizontal slashes of green stranded cotton applied randomly create an interesting striped effect; so as to prevent movement of the stripes, I caught them here and there with a vertical stitch. I later discovered the uses of invisible thread for this technique. By now the reader will be able to identify the method used for the boots.

The background has been left simple so not to distract from the foreground. I cannot stress too much the importance of simplicity when doing decorative stitching. It is perhaps also true to say that, 'A little inaccuracy sometimes saves tons of explanation' (Saki, H. H. Munro).

Detail of the Noddy character.

A TOUCH OF WHIMSY FOR ADULTS

*A clever man commits
no minor blunders.*

Goethe

· ·

PANTRY LADY

The two pieces featured in this chapter have a great deal in common; even if it is simply that many years after their execution I ask myself the question: 'Why the obsession with the rear view of human beings?' At the time of working them, such an enquiry would not have crossed my mind, but looking back I cannot help but feel that I was scared of facing the front view. The implementation of a front view is much more difficult and challenging.

In both the following canvases the figure has been used as a focal point for something else. In this respect alone they opened an exciting door of perspective and execution to me. Certainly the use of a human figure in this way is an easy way to suggest, without actually having to portray realistically, the human form, and it certainly avoids having to work a face!

The source of the subject matter in each case was not entirely original but rather inspired by some work in that marvellous magazine *McCalls Needlework & Crafts*, which is published in the United States six times a year. I would recommend it to anyone as a most inspiring and fascinating magazine that can instil interest, inspire confidence and extend your imagination. I cherish my copies, old and new.

The pantry lady was an ambitious effort quite early in my stitching experiments that owes its origins to a design (shown on page 36) by Cheryl Ruchle in the September 1978 edition of *McCalls*. This splendid design together with detailed instructions for its execution were laid before the reader. At the time of my attempt, my lack of experience and the desire to be original (the latter being a good excuse to cover up the former) produced the slightly altered version pictured opposite. It was great fun to do and has continued to decorate a pine wall facing the kitchen in my house ever since.

The original design was, of course, beautifully drafted and required counting and precision to copy it exactly. By now you will know my thoughts about such replication, hence my rather freer version

For an explanation of the stitches used, the numbers on the diagram relate to the bold numbers in the text.

displays neither meticulous order, symmetry, perfection or even perspective. It is nevertheless an interesting example of trial and error; of what not to do, as much as a recommended solution.

The original McCalls *illustration that inspired the pantry lady.*

Spread across petit-point canvas, the jars in my piece are undisciplined and have been allowed to loom larger than life and reality would have them. Rather than containing jams, jellies and pickles as suggested in the original design, they have been stitched in a variety of colours and textures to represent a rather more varied pantry than one containing only preserves! It is interesting to note that the shadows behind the jars have become somewhat confused as to where they should be. Jars 1, 2, 3 and 4 have their shadows on the wrong side when compared to the other jars. The intention was that light was being shone on the figure from behind so that the shadows behind jars 9 to 16, and 17 to 23 are more accurately how one would expect them to be. I might say that it was not until I sat down to analyse this piece that I noticed this error.

The conscientious embroiderer would no doubt also have ensured that the size of the jars was exactly the same, as well as the lids, and the spaces between each of them. This was an early experiment in perspective: one that did not work and whose ingredients I have never repeated. I have always found that for me to be tied down to a pattern requiring measurement and counting is a chore. Certainly this piece illustrates this! However, it is included to encourage those readers who might share my frustration with such restrictions and to show them that an impressionist version of something symmetrical can be effective. In any event, experimenting with the execution of such pieces as samplers increases your confidence and broadens your experience for future work.

The *McCall's* design had directed the use of Persian yarn and my early pieces will have already shown how effective this is for textured work. I wanted to use up scraps of left-over wools of various colours in a thick gauge as well as some Persian wool remaining from previous pieces. Part of the fun of being creative with your needle and thread is being able to delve into your overcrowded basket of wool to find the right shade, of course, this also serves as economy.

The various jars have been worked as follows. Black French knots **(1)**; multicoloured yellow and mustard French knots **(2)**; vertical strands of white with occasional slashes of black to suggest humbugs **(3)**; purple vertical split satin stitch **(4)**; varying shades of green horizontal split satin stitch **(5)**; vertical strands of white with slashes of red to suggest candy sticks **(6)**; vertical red stranded cotton in split satin stitch **(7)**; tent stitch **(8)** to fade into the border with the shadow; random split satin stitch in a coffee colour **(9)**; green horizontal split satin stitch **(10)**; pink Smyrna cross stitch **(11)** in Persian wool to suggest strawberries. A sweets jar **(12)** of French knots in a gay abandon of mixed colours. The placement of this jar right behind the woman's head was an attempt to be original that did not work; it rather looks as though she is balancing the jar on her head! Yellow tent stitch **(13)**; black French knots **(14)**; green brick stitch **(15)**; red vertical split satin stitch **(16)** in stranded cotton; random stitches in pink wool **(17)**; black French knots **(18)**; purple tent stitch **(19)** in thick-gauge wool, overworked with mauve stranded cotton here and there. The intention here entirely eludes me now, save that the final effect is at least balanced in colour! Another application of vertical stitches in red stranded cotton **(20)**; yellow French knots **(21)**; pink Smyrna cross stitch in Persian wool **(22)**; green tent stitch **(23)** with each interval worked with a vertical tacking stitch over five spaces.

The lids of the jars, also undisciplined and lacking both symmetry and perspective, are worked in slashes of horizontal wool, overstitched here and there with slashes of stranded cotton.

Consistent with my frequently expressed approach, I became impatient with working jars of produce and decided to stock the bottom shelf with various pieces of china and some books. The two cups **(24)** were worked in tent stitch; and the red coffee pot **(25)** effected by slashes of horizontal split satin stitch with its lid divided by vertical stitches over one thread of the canvas. A stack of plates **(26)** was suggested by alternating applications of two shades of brown in tent stitch. A gravy boat **(27)** had its body undercoated and then over-worked in green Persian wool so that it protrudes. I then picked out in red and yellow random stitches a border pattern – or a suggestion of the same. The gravy boat sits on a yellow Persian wool saucer worked for contrast in random Gobelin stitch. The plate behind the gravy boat **(28)** has a tent stitch centre in the colours of the border pattern on the gravy boat, and it is bordered in brown Gobelin stitch over an undercoat for some perspective. The books **(29)** speak for themselves. The casserole dish **(30)** has been worked in the same way as the gravy boat with a pattern suggested by overworking the lid and base in the various shades, and picking out the edges in red and brown tent stitch. The plate behind the casserole dish **(31)** is worked in the same way as the other plate **(28)**. The edge has been picked out with the occasional red tent stitch at random.

I have added a large urn **(32)** to the design, this was intended to add an overall balance to the piece. It is worked in triple brick stitch in Persian wool. The upper surface is in tent stitch to make it less prominent – lip service to perspective at least. The rim of the neck is in Gobelin stitch. The black cat **(33)** has been done in split satin stitch in wool; and the mouse hole **(34)** is worked in tent stitch.

The background **(35)** is entirely worked in tent stitch, and not a terribly even application of that stitch. Here I have repeated a mistake mentioned elsewhere: the tent stitch does not go in the same direction. It is important to keep it not only at an even tension, but also to keep it going in the *same* direction or it will affect the final appearance of the piece. My application of it here was an undisciplined one as I worked some rows in the reverse direction. No doubt the excitement of working on three-dimensional experiments made such execution tiring, but you must remember to see a piece as a whole and realise that obvious mistakes will spoil the final effect.

One way to avoid being bored by the background, is to do a little at a time; alternating between that and the decorative pieces. In so doing, however, you must also remember that to avoid distortion of the canvas you should avoid working solely on one area at the expense of the other areas. Working in various parts of the canvas rather than in one section only will assist you in keeping the piece relatively in shape as you proceed.

The shelves **(36)** are worked in split satin stitch in Persian wool. The woman's hair **(37)** is a clockwise application of Gobelin stitch; first from the centre for her crown, then around the edge over six or so squares for her chignon. Her blouse (38) is in rows of diamond stitch worked alternately horizontally and vertically to achieve a flowered look. The centres are in Smyrna cross stitch. The individual long stitches within the diamond have not been executed with any great precision to give the blouse a looser appearance. The cuffs and neckline have stranded-cotton slashes to give added interest.

The white apron (39) was added to provide interest of texture and also to straighten the skirt a little. My enthusiasm had warped the canvas to the point where nothing I did could bring the bottom section of her body back into line. Even now there is a slight sway to the right that artistic licence might suggest to be a 'gammy' leg beneath the skirt. I seem to remember I tried stretching the piece myself at this stage in an effort to rectify the problem, but to no avail. Hence I decided that by covering up the extremities of the skirt (which drew attention to the lean to the right) I might overcome the problem to a degree. I think it has assisted. The apron is worked by horizontal applications of split satin stitch in white Persian wool and the edges trimmed in grey wool to avoid her body merging into the background with its white wall. Her skirt (40) was worked in rows of five or six tent stitches in alternate directions to give the surface a rough tweedy look.

The floor (41) is supposed to suggest weatherboards in rows of horizontal Gobelin stitch. The skirting-board (42) has been added to give extra perspective and interest to the background. The horizontal insets are in split satin stitch and the vertical sections are in Gobelin stitch.

As I have indicated already, the canvas was fairly badly distorted at the end of this exercise and to make matters worse when it came back from the framer it was a disaster. The shelves were askew and all the vertical surfaces had a lean to them. The lean in her skirt had been made much worse. I recall ripping the brown paper from the back in desperation and panic; thankful at least to discover that the framer had used staples to secure the canvas to its backing and not glue. Never allow glue near the back of a piece when it is to be mounted – it is then impossible to remove the backing without damaging your piece.

I was forced by this disaster into stretching it back into shape myself before finding another framer. The method I used then is one I have continued to find useful and effective, and I explain it on pages 111–112. Necessity is, indeed, the mother of invention.

HAL'S LADY

The romantic view of a garden drawing your eyes beyond the mono-tone of the interior was a direct result of my own experience as a gardener's assistant. This piece is very precious to me since it was an early attempt to create a tribute to a special friend on his birthday. This friend has since died, and it was among his final wishes that my creation be returned to me. It was, and I treasure it.

I like to think that it was the culmination of many lessons, and an example of how exciting it can be to work on a simple idea and develop it to suit your own purpose.

It was also in many ways a lesson for future pieces. First, I must acknowledge that the basic design for the piece was adapted by me from a design for a quilt in the same edition of *McCalls* that contained the previous design. A comparison of the two will show you that the final product is in no sense a replica of the quilted hanging – except, perhaps, in so far as it has a wavy window line!

I had been on my hands and knees in Hal Sarah's garden and mowed his lawns on a regular basis, as my job required me to do. An enjoyable part of the job was spent sipping tea, eating cakes and biscuits or imbibing a glass of wine or whisky at the end of the day. Gardeners enjoy communing with clients as well as with nature! In no time at all we became good friends and always enjoyed a chat. Besides being a cheerful person, Hal was also a very talented dress designer who had won a special award in the annual Gown of the Year competition. His modesty prevented him dragging out his scrap-books and memorabilia to boast and all he would say was that his gown had been a 'shirtmaker with a jewelled belt'. His speciality was beading and exquisite stitching of every sort and I would marvel at his elaborate workshop, which he also used as a comfortable sitting-room, surround-ed by fascinating fabrics, mannequins, sequins, diamantés, beads and myriads of memories of a creative past.

I was inspired by the generosity and fun in this man to create something special for him for his sixtieth birthday. Hence in the piece illustrated opposite, I set out to recognise and enshrine the beauty and peace of his garden, which I knew well. I also wanted to frame it with a subtle hint at what I did not know, but imagined would be exquisite: his winning gown. The whole piece would be a tribute to friendship and a gesture of thanks for this creative man.

What finally emerged from my needle, thread and a panic to produce perfection was a mish-mash of mistakes. I had intended initially to have the maiden in a monotone to highlight the garden and to act simply as a frame for the piece. Accordingly, I had decided that everything but the garden should be kept simple so that the former would be prominent. But the woman in the jewelled belt is far from simple, as you can see.

I had intended that her skirt and bodice would be worked in the most basic stitches in muted shades to allow the jewelled belt to be obvious. I had also intended that the draped curtain would be equally straightforward so not to distract the eye from the belt or the garden. In these respects my intentions were not effected at all – and in a sense what one sees is the result of a giant mistake. I had sketched the design on to Etamine canvas with a pencil and darkened it, for ease of working, with a ballpoint pen. This made things much easier for my tired eyes to see. Hence the first efforts at achieving simplicity worked quite well. The curtain (1) was worked, as by now you will recognise, in a combination of encroaching Gobelin and split satin stitches in pale pink thick-gauge wool, the stitches lying horizontally. The intervals of the folds have been worked in a similar stitch in pale pink stranded cotton to allow an appropriate contrast. The critic might suggest that these folds should have been darker to suggest reality, but simplicity and monotone was my aim. The skirt (7) was worked in blocks of tent stitch worked in opposite directions to achieve a pleated look and to provide tone on tone contrast without allowing it to leap into prominence. (I have used this tone-on-tone pleated look elsewhere to suggest fabric.)

Again, I must say that this object was not achieved at all! By now you will want to know why I did not achieve my aims. The answer must also be a warning to any student of creative needlepoint: never use a ballpoint pen, or any drawing implement that is not dye-fast on fabric. Disaster struck me when I collected the piece from the dry-cleaner prior to having it framed – the ink had run and introduced an unwelcome rhapsody in blue that certainly relieved the pale pink monotony! I have since found that there are water-fast and dye-fast pens available. 'Bic' or 'Pentel' pens are safe to use. Art shops and suppliers will advise you as to safe drawing instruments. Remember pieces will be wet both at the stretching stage and if you have it dry-cleaned (when they are subject to chemicals). I have found that pale shades do discolour as you work and dry-cleaning at some stage before framing is, therefore, essential.

The dilemma was whether to discard a piece that had gone all wrong and to start again, or to try to fix it somehow. Here was the best lesson for the beginner. There is absolutely no point in discarding something that has taken months to do – the uniqueness of a piece cannot ever be successfully repeated. One must exercise patience and ingenuity and try to create calm from mayhem. Hence the final skirt, bodice and curtain and their embellishment was not what I had set out to do, but I was able to make a success of a failure. Such a challenge is not necessarily a happy one at the time, but teaches one a lesson in flexibility and confidence.

It also teaches one that it is a good idea to leave unexplained to admiring enquirers what your intention or design was. In that way you do not need to experience any embarrassment for the mistakes that

The page from McCalls *showing the quilt that gave me the idea for Hal's lady.*

have intervened. Of course, in any event, the related adventure of a rescued piece makes good dinner party conversation!

If you study the numbered diagram you might be interested to begin with the cured mistakes first. The numbers 1, 2, 6, 7, 8 and 10 show where there was an abundance of blue ink to be hidden. In the case of the curtains **(1)** I have abandoned simplicity and perspective and worked some simple, loose daisies over blue spots that, while robbing the curtain of its natural look, add some extra interest to its framing of the garden.

For an explanation of the stitches used, the numbers on the diagram relate to the bold numbers in the text.

Areas 6 and 7 were the real problems, since the staining was very obvious in these places. The good old French knot came to my rescue. Applied thickly in pearl cotton over the simple pearl cotton skirt they add a tone-on-tone interest without too much distraction. If anything it gives an extra perspective to the piece that makes up for the disappointment at having to interfere with the initial texture of the simpler design that you can still see in places (7). To add balance and prevent the blocks of French knots from giving the skirt a heavy, contrived look, I added various scattered daisies and flowers (8) to link the areas covered with French knots (6) together. These were worked in loose buttonhole stitch and French knots highlighted with a pink metallic thread as well. This was to invite the eye to see the skirt as a whole, rather than in chunks.

I think the intention here does work as, from a distance, the framing of the garden is still effective, while on closer inspection the texture appears appliquéd – a suggestion, perhaps, of brocade. At least if your imagination does not stretch that far, you will agree that distraction is avoided and, at the very least, the skirt remains creamy pink rather than blue!

The bodice (9) had initially been worked in pink stranded cotton in horizontal Gobelin stitch to give the appearance of simplicity and to contrast with and allow prominence to the jewelled belt. Blue stains had necessitated action. I chose to work random daisies in pink stranded cotton across the obvious surfaces, adding a pink metallic thread French knot here and there for the stamens. Again the problem was solved without being too distracting.

The bow (11) was enlarged to cover up another problem area; while sacrificing reality, since it disturbs the perspective, this adds some interest to the frame for the garden. The bow is actually worked in thick-gauge pink wool in horizontal Gobelin stitch to cover the surface and then outlined in pink metallic thread in a tacking stitch. The bulkiness of the hair (10), worked in stranded cotton in split satin stitch, adds a contrast of texture and a third dimension anticipated by the bow.

The jewelled belt (12) was purposely enlarged and elongated into a peak to cover up more blue stain. It is worked in metallic thread and is simply made up of a roughly worked daisy atop a few rows of cross stitch, with the odd French knot and then outlined in tacking stitch to define its limits.

I later discovered the fun one could have by adding beads, sequins and diamantés, but at this stage of my development I was still either naive or purist about stitching; it does not really matter which since, as it stands, it is almost over the top without any extra embellishment!

The remaining areas in the numbered diagram disclose relatively successful attempts to achieve my purpose without being blue. The tie back for the curtain (2) was worked vertically in thick-gauge pink wool in Gobelin stitch; bordered in long stitches to allow protuberance.

Simple but effective. The carpet (3) has been worked in stranded cotton in tent stitch, which against the other surfaces that tend to protrude, gives correct perspective to achieve the third dimension. That is, you expect the carpet to be further away!

I added a creamy pink cat (5) with a pink metallic thread collar. The cat is worked in Persian wool in split satin stitch over an undercoat to give him some extra dimension. He is staring at a wall panel (13) that is worked in pink pearl cotton Smyrna cross and outlined in tacking stitch. This all adds interesting texture consistent with my principles of perspective and dimension.

Areas of the garden (14) are worked respectively in tent stitch and French knots (15), save for the daisies (16) that I worked randomly. The blue and cream flowers are supposed to be lupins and the clustered red ones are intended to be geraniums. Hal Sarah's garden was colourful, varied and full of lovely geraniums and pelargoniums. Perspective was sacrificed for effect here, as the geraniums and lupins appear to leap through the panes of glass one would expect in the windows. Artistic licence yet again! The background (14) was worked in blocks of colour, as the mood struck, to create the impression of bushes and foliage; I had no particular design in mind, save an attempt to create a scene by applications of light and shade. The need to view the piece from afar to get the distant view was much required at this stage.

The window frames (4) were worked in Gobelin stitch, and when I stretched the piece it was very difficult to ensure that the frames were actually straight. I did not allow obsession about that to dictate the final result in this case, and I never do. Near enough in this respect, often needs to be good enough, so not to disturb the balance of the rest of the piece.

The perspective and depth was enhanced by ensuring that when framed, it had a triple mount in complementary shades. Overall the final result was very pleasing, despite the problems encountered on the way. Of all my work to date, I find this to be the most admired by onlookers – I often smile to myself when I recall the near disaster it was and continue to be encouraged by the challenge presented to me by a mistake upon my journey with the needle and thread. I would encourage you to resort to the same philosophy in your own creative adventure.

·· 6 ··

TRADITIONAL PIECES WITH A DIFFERENCE

The essential in daring is to know
how far one can go too far.

Jean Cocteau

. . . .

Creative stitching does not need to be restricted to naive printed canvases or require you to make your own designs. It can be effective if used with restraint on traditional canvases designed for conventional stitching. The four examples in this chapter are some of my attempts to introduce an element of individualism into such pieces.

SWISS COUNTRY WEDDING

The first piece illustrated is a well known, semi-naive picture entitled 'Heiteres Landleben' from Rico-Gobelin designs. This looks fabulous when simply worked in tent stitch without further embellishment. I like to think, nevertheless, that a few little decorative touches here and there add extra interest and appeal. Certainly my visitors seem to think so. By now your trained eye will be able to identify the basic stitches I have used to embellish it. I shall therefore only identify them generally and let you work out the details for yourself.

The smoke emanating from the little train has been worked in the stitch I used for Santa's hat and the rabbit's tail; the clouds are split satin stitch; the various trees in the field are worked in French knots (some in cotton, some in wool). The trees immediately behind the

buildings are worked variously, from left to right, in bargello, horizontal long stitch, random Gobelin stitch, Smyrna cross stitch and variations of brick stitch and French knots. The buildings themselves are picked out in cotton and wool in Gobelin or long stitch in both the vertical and horizontal plane for variety. Metallic threads here and there (in the various flowers and the sun) help to bring the picture to life and catch the light. The tree behind the fisherman that frames the piece is an early attempt at leaf stitch, this lends perspective (as do some of the bushes in the left-hand corner below the fisherman). Notice the corn bundles near the fisherman's head, these are borrowed from the sampler described in the first chapter. The fisherman's left side is worked in Gobelin stitch; the children behind him are picked out in Gobelin stitch and French knots and the sail on the yacht (given a figure 7 for some reason that now escapes me) has been padded and worked over in Gobelin stitch in white cotton. The cow has been worked in wool in split satin stitch, while the pig is in cotton and worked in Gobelin stitch. The splash of flowers between the two are my own addition and consist of the daisies I have already described; they add a surreal touch and display my new found creativity! The bold pink, maroon and white flowers against a background of blue lupins will now be familiar. Again a touch of metallic thread adds lustre.

The pièce de resistance is the bride, who seems to be marrying Charlie Chaplin! Her gown has been worked in pink metallic thread, oversewn with pale pink pearl cotton in chain stitch linked both vertically and horizontally to suggest lace (I developed this technique further, see pages 66 and 106). Her peroxide blonde hair of French knots is topped with a veil of loosely worked chain stitch in stranded cotton; the individual loops of the chain have then been teased out so as to suggest netting and caught here and there with the invisible thread that my friend Hal Sarah had introduced me to. The tiara is a series of random long stitches in silver metallic thread; this is also worked at random in the body of the veil in tent stitch to abide by proper perspective and lend lustre. Her bouquet is made up of French knots of cotton, wool and metallic thread. The page-boy and girl will be, by now, self-explanatory. My favourite touch is the large rooster at the right-hand bottom corner. His comb is made up of stranded cotton in split satin stitch, as are parts of his body, which is also in tent stitch, with a tail of chain stitch. His feet are stranded cotton slashes to lend balance.

As long as one bears in mind the principle not to be too smart or clever and to exercise some restraint in fiddling with a conventional piece, you can have a lot of fun by stamping it with your own individuality.

WILLOW PATTERN FAN

The second traditional piece is a willow pattern fan – a hand-painted canvas by Princely Needlecraft – worked mainly in tent stitch. This piece is, from the stitching point of view, unremarkable save for the use of unworked canvas to add to its texture. Elsewhere (pages 87 and 101) I have touched upon the interest that is added by treating the canvas as an acceptable surface in itself. Perhaps you will agree that the fan is a good example of this principle since being able to see the canvas in the folds of the fan's spokes suggests raffia or some other appropriate texture. The stitching of this area that a purist would insist upon would, to my mind, ruin it. Metallic thread here and there, a touch of Gobelin stitch and my insistence that the framer mount the piece as I wanted it, has made it a little different from the usual and a welcome addition to my sitting-room.

MEDIEVAL WALLHANGING

This piece was worked from yet another kit, again from Paternayan Bros. I was attracted by its *Saturday Evening Post* look and its pastel shades; it is a far cry from traditional medieval pictures. On this occasion I have added beads to pick out the predominant areas and add interest to the final product. The piece is not presented in the exact chronological order of my learning process but, as I mentioned in the previous chapter, Hal Sarah had taught me about invisible thread and in particular its use in sewing on beads and sequins. The ladies in this piece are therefore embellished in this way: pearls on a hat and red crystals on the collar and cuffs give extra interest to an already romantic scene. The red hat is worked in Smyrna cross stitch to add dimension and texture. There is also a mistake that deserves comment. The lady in pink wears a veil. That is my own addition, a cure for a coffee stain acquired from a careless cup in the course of creation.

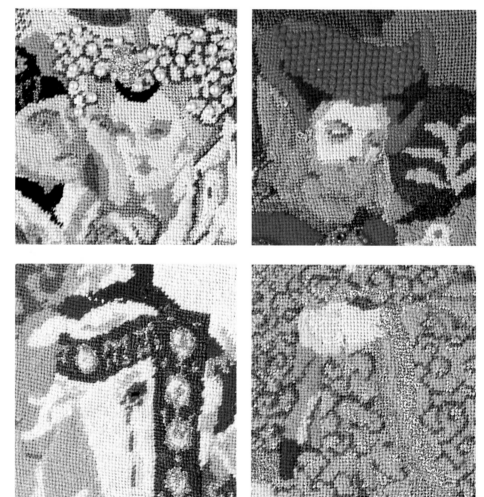

Details of the wallhanging show how different textures have been obtained by the use of different threads and stitches.

CEZANNE STILL LIFE

This picture, based on a painting by Cezanne, (from a Penelope canvas by Rico-Gobelin) is worked mostly in tent stitch in the traditional manner and stitched in a combination of stranded cotton, pearl cotton and thick-gauge wool to vary the texture and to give a hint of the third dimension.

The fruit in the foreground is worked mostly in thick-gauge wool, whereas that in the middle-ground is in stranded cotton. The wine glass is also in thick-gauge wool against a background of various shades of stranded cotton in both petit-point and gros-point. The bunch of leaves in the right-hand corner is entirely in thick-gauge wool against a background of stranded cotton. Behind that are touches of beige petit-point stranded cotton, against gros-point stranded cotton.

The bowl of the fruit dish is worked in a combination of wool in green and pearl cotton in white, this creates its own contrasts and allows it to predominate against the background in grey and mauve stranded cotton in both gros-point and petit-point with a splash of mauve thick-gauge wool (above the yellow fruit) adding texture and dimension. The base of the fruit dish is worked in thick-gauge pearl cotton to give it prominence, fading into pale green and white stranded cotton petit-point. This allows the base of the dish to be deep set behind the shiny red apple immediately to its right. This apple is worked in stranded cotton in gros-point, except for a patch of thick-gauge red pearl cotton in the centre to give a sheen. The red apple in the foreground is worked entirely in thick-gauge wool in gros-point, while the green and grey piece of fruit behind it is in stranded cotton. Where the fruit and background meet, the canvas is worked in petit-point to reinforce the feeling of depth. In the same way, the folds of the cloth at the base of the fruit dish are stitched in thick-gauge wool and stranded cotton in both gros-point and petit-point in shades of grey, green and white; these reinforce the three dimensional feeling. The bone-handled knife adds to this effect. It is worked in thick-gauge wool in gros-point against a background of petit-point in stranded cotton, the effect is to throw it forward. The technique is repeated inside the fruit dish, with the piece of fruit to the rear in stranded cotton gros-point against a petit-point stranded-cotton background. The three pieces of fruit in the middle and foreground are in thick-gauge wool, as is the mauve right-hand corner and edge of the bowl; while the three grapes are given even further predominance by a Gobelin-stitch overcoat. Otherwise restraint abounds!

It is worth noting that this experiment did expose the canvas in spots – I can even see one or two missing stitches! I think this lends its own charm to the piece. I suggest that you may lend artistry to the traditional stitching of a conventional piece by an innovative use of threads alone.

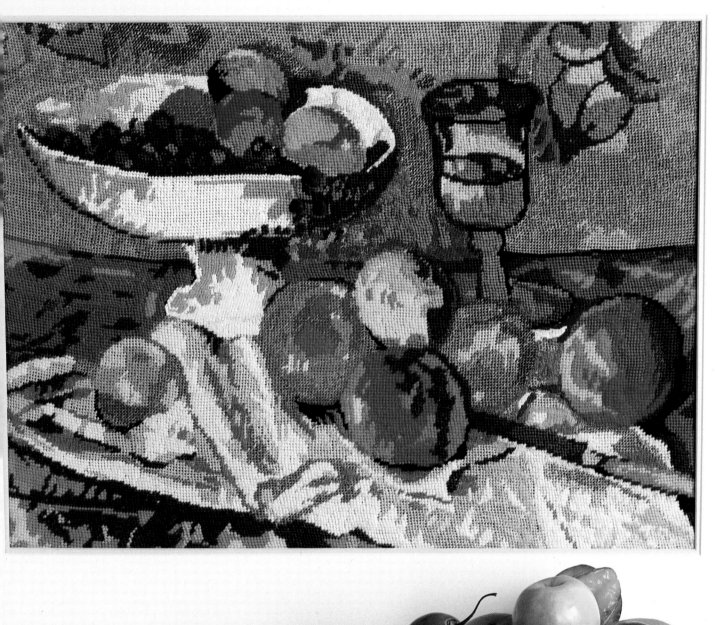

7

THE ALICE COLLECTION

'And what is the use of a book?'
thought Alice
'Without pictures or conversations'.

Lewis Carroll: Alice in Wonderland

Life, what is it but a dream?

Lewis Carroll: Through the Looking-Glass

· ·

I write in 1991. It is fitting and appropriate for me to recognise here that 1990 was the International Year of literacy; it was also the year that marked 125 years of Lewis Carroll's book *Alice in Wonderland*. This chapter features five pieces of my own design and realisation, wholly inspired by this remarkable man's works and in particular by Alice's dreams, which remain magnetic and powerful for children of all ages.

Four of the five pieces were based on the amazing sketches of Sir John Tenniel who illustrated Carroll's work and transformed these dreams and word pictures into reality. All of these pieces were displayed in Melbourne in 1990 as part of an exhibition paying homage to Lewis Carroll's creation.

Alice in Wonderland as a book had an indelible effect on my growing up. It has similarly affected my adventure in stitching: my needle yearned to bring these pictures to life in colour and textures. I searched in vain for appropriate canvases. I ultimately decided to draw my own, mostly by reference to some reproductions of Tenniel's illustrations taken from a colouring book used and loved by my eldest son, Christopher. I carefully sketched on to Etamine canvas my favourite images and worked them with great pleasure. They were not all worked at once, of course, but over a period of many years. I have plans for more, but in describing these completed pieces that have stretched

through my most productive period of stitching to date, I share with you their challenge and, I like to think, accomplishment.

It is in these pieces that all of the lessons I had learnt from my earlier work came together, and they inspired me to look beyond cartoons to achieve at least a hint of reality. A life of dreams reflects a person's dreams of life, and these tapestries encapsulate both aspects of their author.

WHITE RABBIT IN A GREAT HURRY

The first piece in my Alice adventure is illustrated on page 57. It is the lid of a padded box that was, again, an Easter gift, hence its shape. It was based on an exquisite illustration that I had come across thanks to an Easter card from a friend. Entitled 'The White Rabbit, splendidly dressed, came trotting along in a great hurry', it had been illustrated by Gwynedd M. Hudson for a modern version of *Alice in Wonderland* published by Hodder and Stoughton.

The Easter card that was the basis for my piece showing the white rabbit in a great hurry.

The padded box was stitched together by my friend Val Landman after I had sketched this design on to Etamine canvas and coloured it in with needle and thread. In fairness I should remind you of a common mistake of mine at this stage so that you can avoid it. I did not allow a sufficiently large unworked border to enable my friend to work with when completing the covered box, hence you may notice a little puckering round the edges and near the white rabbit's ears. Fortunately my error did not prevent Val Landman from hiding my sins and creating a piece of silk from a sow's ear. The finished piece is about 28 cm by 20 cm (11 in by 8 in) and much treasured.

You will now be familiar with the tight applications of satin stitch in various shades of cream to achieve shading of the rabbit's fur **(1)**. Thick-gauge wool has been used instead of Persian yarn; a correspondingly coarser texture is achieved. I have always thought the white rabbit was more a hare than a rabbit anyway! The tail **(2)** is done in the same way as the Easter bunny and Santa's pom-pom.

The neckerchief or cravat **(3)** has been undercoated in cream wool and then stitched over in a loose chain stitch of varying sizes and consistency to suggest movement and bulk. The decorative cuff **(4)** has been undercoated to give it prominence and then embellished with metallic thread slashes and French knots. His split-satin stitch hand

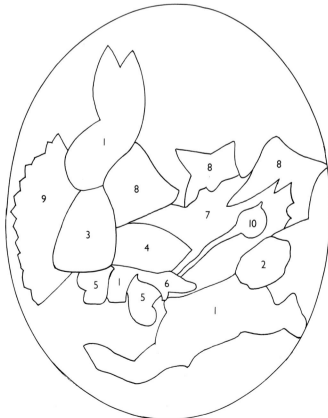

For an explanation of the stitches used, the numbers on the diagram relate to the bold numbers in the text.

clutches at yellow kid gloves **(5)** worked in the same stitch but highlighted in slashes of a darker colour. The froth of lace **(6)** emanating from the cuff in the original was represented yet again by some undisciplined use of chain stitch, teased out here and there with the needle and caught with an invisible thread. Exercise of restraint has kept the idea in check. The jacket **(7)** is effected in pink Persian wool in tent stitch. The pale pink background is similarly stitched, except that I used pearl cotton. The rabbit's collar and coat-tails **(8)** are yet again a mass of wildly abandoned French knots in metallic thread, with random, silver, roughly slashed daisies to give a contrast and richness.

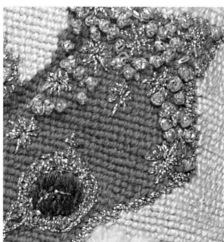

Details of the stitches show the textural variations in the piece.

The fan **(9)** is worked in a herringbone pattern by alternating applications of stranded cotton, but allowed to be fairly loose to prevent it from becoming too contrived. After all, the rabbit is in a hurry and light fabrics would hardly remain tight or unaffected by the breeze. The suggestion of movement is reinforced by my own insertion of a watch and chain **(10)** flying from a pocket, worked in a gold metallic thread chain stitch and left fairly loose.

WHITE RABBIT HERALDING THE ARRIVAL OF THE QUEEN OF HEARTS

This is the first of my Alice pieces based on Tenniel's original illustrations.

Tenniel's illustration was the basis for the design for the lid of the box.

The White Rabbit's fur, has been realized in a manner that will **(1)** by now, be familiar to you – split satin stitch in thick-gauge wool. Notice that I totally forgot to include the half dozen black whiskers. You might like to ponder as to how best they would have been effected. The rabbit's eye could also have been a little more sophisticated, but in my defence I say that this was an early piece (circa 1984).

The collar **(2)** has been only roughly approximated in random applications of chain stitch that edge Gobelin-stitched areas emanating from the neck. The stitching was kept loose to give it prominence for the appropriate dimension and perspective. The blue bow **(3)** is in Gobelin stitch outlined in thin-gauge pearl cotton and sits atop a jerkin-type sleeve in metallic thread in tent stitch against a lining of maroon tent stitch. The outline of the jerkin and sleeve has been stitched over in yellow pearl cotton. The green and gold cuff **(4)** is made to protrude by repeated loose applications of tent stitch and is allowed to remain undisciplined for effect. The scroll **(5)** is made up of pale pink pearl cotton in adaptations of split satin stitch against a background of deep pink tent stitch in Persian wool. The seal **(6)** hangs from the scroll.

It will not be difficult for you, by now, to analyse the rest for yourself.

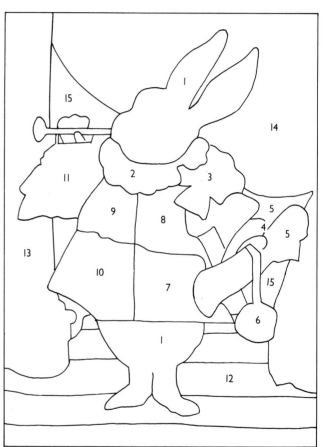

For an explanation of the stitches used, the numbers on the diagram relate to the bold numbers in the text.

The body of the jerkin **(7)**, **(8)**, **(9)**, **(10)** was worked in variations on the theme of metallic threads and pearl cotton. In an effort to reverse contrasts, I employed these two threads and worked in tent stitch together with undercoated Gobelin stitch. The banner **(11)** was worked in the same way as the jerkin and the most individual achievement of perspective (and the most fun) is the tassel, which has only been worked in undisciplined stitches of metallic gold thread.

The staircase **(12)** was a challenge: a decision had to be made as to how a third dimension for the background could be achieved in a

decorative stitch that would not overtake the foreground. You may judge whether the solution was successful or not. To get the effect, I worked the surface of the stairs in brick stitch alternating the direction of the stitch and dividing it every so often either by horizontal tacking stitches in gold metallic thread or vertical stitches of wool. The horizontal brick stitch is over three or four squares, while the vertical is only over two squares. This creates a slight difference in texture, as a velvet carpet on stairs would be affected by the play of light from different angles or as feet treading on its surface would leave it. The grey stone pillar **(13)** is an application of Persian wool in tight fashion; a marvellous medium to suggest textures. The plinth has been worked in split satin stitch; the flutes are all in Gobelin stitch and the indented sections in single horizontal stitches in a slightly darker shade of grey. The background **(15)** is executed in tent stitch and the green drape **(14)** is a thick-gauge pearl cotton worked in different directions for each fold; that is to say, tent stitch in the horizontal plane alternated with tent stitch in the vertical plane (this I work by turning the canvas through 90° and then stitching in the usual way). The black interval in the folds was an attempt to ensure that the observer got the message! I think now it need not have been so obvious. My future drapes tend not to employ this method.

ALICE IN THE CORRIDOR

This piece was based on Tenniel's drawing of Alice in the corridor gazing in awe and wonderment as the white rabbit toddles off in a great hurry. It is my version of this classic portrait. The completed work is about 25 cm by 21 cm (10 in by 8½ in). Artistic licence, and apologies to Sir John Tenniel, must be offered in explanation of one change from his original illustration **(9)**. The white rabbit in my picture is, in fact, making for a garden of French knots!

The white rabbit **(8)**, bathed in light from the open garden door, hurries towards it resplendent in a pink stranded-cotton coat worked from the centre in Gobelin stitch with a pink metallic threaded collar and two French knots in metallic thread for buttons. His body is, predictably, worked in split satin stitch in cream Persian wool, he has a fluffy tail worked as previously described (page 18) and this time he has whiskers too! Note that, in fact, he is not defined with too much labour: his legs are merely suggestions; an application of already discussed need for restraint. He has left behind his fan **(13)**, which is made up of random slashes of pink stranded cotton interspersed with touches of metallic thread.

On his right, the wall boards of the corridor **(7)** are uniformly stitched in Gobelin stitch with brown stranded cotton over two canvas holes; this technique displays intervals of canvas to great effect. Any attempt to stitch the divisions would be much less effective than allowing the exposed canvas play its own simple part in the picture. This piece was worked on traditional beige Penelope canvas and the sight of the latter here and there through the stitches is both purposeful and effective. The suggestion of a central railing has been added in vertical Gobelin stitch to assist with the perspective of the piece. The same comment about the canvas may be made in relation to the floor **(6)**, which has been worked in tent stitch and happily leaves exposed canvas edges to great effect, I think. Without being supplemented by extra strands a thread of stranded cotton does not ever fully cover a surface.

Alice's black slipper and sock **(5)** is done in Gobelin stitch in stranded cotton. The wall behind her **(4)** has been worked in a darker shade since it is further from the light and one would expect it to be darker. It may well have been more effective (and very clever) to make this area black and to grade the brown towards the door gradually from dark to light for a more realistic picture. As I have previously remarked, however, cottons are unfortunately not shaded subtlely from light to dark (it was probably also the case that in 1985 my artistry was not really up to such refinement). In relation to light and shade, you will note that the vaulted ceiling **(10)** has a similar effect of getting darker – an attempt in the interests of artistic consciousness.

Yet another of Tenniel's illustrations that was to inspire my work!

Alice's frock **(3)** was worked in slanting or encroaching Gobelin stitch in stranded cotton in the appropriate direction to suggest the material folding and with shadows worked in a darker thread in tent or Gobelin stitch here and there. The puffed sleeves are in the same cotton but worked in rows of horizontal Gobelin stitch. French knots edge the sleeve above slashes of darker-still cotton.

The pinafore **(11)** was an experiment, both in shade and application of chain stitch, that worked. I wanted to suggest a lacy look and also felt the need to make the garment contrast yet blend with the whole. White would have been overpowering and incorrect given the basic hues of the picture. The grey chain stitch has been worked at random, large and small stitches linked horizontally and vertically and left loose to suggest movement with Alice's body that, one imagines, has just prior to this moment jerked backwards in consternation! In any event, shadows might make her white pinny appear grey.

For an explanation of the stitches used, the numbers on the diagram relate to the bold numbers in the text.

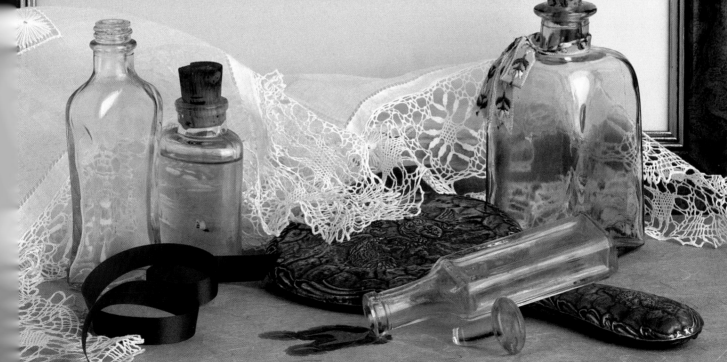

The flesh **(2)** is, of course, worked in petit-point in three strands of stranded cotton. The hands were too difficult for me, so I gave her gloves **(12)** of stranded cotton worked in Gobelin stitch with creases of tent stitch in brown to divide the fingers. Her face was also a challenge, especially the colours for the lines of the eyes, lips and cheeks. I settled for a suggestion of pink. From a distance they work, even if up close I am not quite so sure. Alice's hair **(1)** has been carefully overworked in split satin stitch with cream stranded cotton in various shades, taking care to avoid straight lines.

The border repeats rows of Smyrna cross stitch and the whole thing is double mounted in complementary shades.

This is a favourite piece of mine, as much for its simplicity as its subtlety. I like to think that it is a good example of restraint as the number of decorative stitches actually used in the piece is really very limited indeed.

COURT SCENE

In contrast to the previous Alice pieces, the court scene is far from subtle or simple, and it took me in excess of four years to complete. It is, of course, loosely based on Tenniel's original illustration shown opposite. The completed canvas is about 94 cm by 56 cm (38 in by 22 in).

My major concern at the outset, having sketched the subject on to my large piece of Etamine canvas with a pentel pen was whether to work it on a frame. The other problem was just where to start: it all looked rather forbidding and scary, although it was also exciting to contemplate the challenge of it. I did initially attach it to a frame on a stand when working a great deal of the lower half, but for reasons I have previously discussed, I eventually removed it. It was especially frustrating not being able to see the whole canvas as each part came to life. It was also important for me to balance the colours and I could not do that when part of the canvas was out of sight! The pleasure and challenge of colouring in Tenniel's black and white version was, in itself, a special treat for the child in me!

I have numbered the diagram with the actual chronology of stitching in mind, as I believe it is constructive for you to observe the actual development over a lengthy period. It was, of course, also a period in which some of the previously illustrated pieces were executed so that each piece was a lesson for and an experiment in the other. I will leave it to you to guess the borrowed bits!

Space will not permit a meticulous analysis of every detail in the piece, but much of it you will already be able to identify for yourself; the following areas may be of interest. The rather sonky-looking guard **(1)** watching the knave from his position by the witness box exhibits the studied precision that my early enthusiasm dictated. Note the tightness of the stitches here compared to those say in the rabbit **(12)**, or the King **(13)** and Queen **(11)**. As the work progressed, my fear of it diminished and the finished effect became obviously more relaxed, spontaneous and less contrived. The guard's leg is worked in grey stranded cotton in Gobelin stitch and kept even and tight to suggest the sheen of a silk stocking. This protrudes from breeches of a darker hue also done in stranded cotton in a herringbone pattern of rows of

Tenniel's original illustration of the court scene.

alternating tent stitch. His jerkin is self-explanatory save that the half
hearts are worked in Gobelin stitch in Persian wool, stranded cotton
and metallic thread respectively from top to bottom to allow a contrast
of texture within the contrast of colours. Note the back of his jacket;
vertical pleats of Gobelin stitch over two or three holes interspersed
with gold tent stitch intervals allow a satisfactory contrast both with his
breeches and his sleeve. The latter is given a third dimension of its own
by being worked in a loose long stitch of Persian wool, sufficiently
multiplied to give it bulk and a proper perspective. His white gloved
hand clutches a 'hearty spear' entirely worked in metallic threads over
an undercoat.

Notice that it is difficult to keep a straight line, such as the handle
of this spear, when it is worked at an angle to the edge of the canvas.
Try it, you will see what I mean. I did not concern myself too much
with it and still do not allow straight lines to become an obsession in my
work. The best time to deal with such a problem is after all the

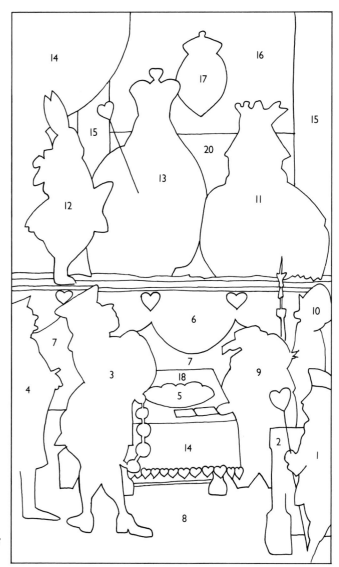

*For an explanation of the
stitches used, the numbers
on the diagram relate to the
bold numbers in the text.*

surrounding surfaces are completed. That allows you to cheat a little, by sewing through a neighbouring section rather than through blank canvas, which creates the problem in the first place. The collar is worked as the collar of the white rabbit, previously described on pages 61–63, but this time the chain stitch is in pearl cotton over an undercoat of Persian wool to create a soft, yet structured, appearance. His hair is worked in strands of thick-gauge wool, which I allowed to be loose to give a third dimension. The hair tidily shows beneath his forage cap, which was worked, as the mood struck, in variations of Gobelin and tent stitch.

The witness box **(2)** will be an obvious recipe by now, but effective use of Gobelin stitch on the exterior is contrasted with a basic bargello stitch in stranded cotton, edged with intervals of metallic thread on the interior, so that it is interesting but flat by contrast.

The pompous, self-righteous Knave of Hearts **(3)** (who is accused of having stolen the tarts) needed to be vain and splendid. I particularly enjoyed bringing him to life.

His hair was an experiment away from the texture of the guard and the effects I had previously used in other pieces. I wanted the page-boy chignon to stand out and so worked it in Persian wool in Gobelin stitch over an undercoat. I gradually changed the direction of the thread to turn the corner and go in the opposite direction, covering and recovering the surface until it was as I wanted it. I also worked this effect in the vertical plane for the bulk of his hair but, to allow for contrasts and variety, I have introduced the odd tent stitch in the same direction. Even when these stitches are the same colour, they allow for very interesting textural contrasts. These are not necessarily noticeable from a distance, but some surprises should be kept in store for those who wish to study a piece more closely! His hair protrudes from a colourful cap, the details of which I shall let you work out for yourself. The top of the jacket is mostly worked in grey tent stitch relieved by lettuce green slashes of Gobelin stitch; this enables the circlet of green leaves to predominate against an inset background of grey. Touches of red and gold tell their own story to the experienced eye. Red metallic thread enhances his back, which is divided from the bloused sleeve by a band of dark green and red tent stitch with embossed leaves worked in metallic thread, Persian wool and pearl thread that are undercoated and raised up with Gobelin stitch. The collar and the belt are structured and predictably repetitive. The skirt of the jacket is constructed in long stitch of various lengths and contrasting colours interspersed with a gold band of lettuce green Smyrna cross stitch. The red and green band across the bottom is made up of Smyrna cross stitch in green metallic thread alternated with red long stitch. All in all, a tailored look is created by contrast to the bloused upper surface.

His pantaloons have been worked in tent stitch on the left and Gobelin stitch on the right, undercoated to allow for a third dimension. The stockings were worked in pearl cotton that has been given a tight

application. The knave's shoes are worked over an undercoat in tent stitch and topped with copper metallic thread buckles of random long stitch to complete the effect. A copper chain worked in the same way attests to his imprisoned status!

The rather unattractive guard **(4)** on the left of the picture is notable for two reasons. First, you will notice on the extreme left a band of long stitch appears all the way down. This is because I had allowed excitement and enthusiasm to interfere with precision. Upon completion and stretching I found this area was left unstitched, and to compensate and straighten the canvas before it was mounted I had to colour it in accordingly. The purist would have painstakingly stitched these surfaces in the appropriate stitches. I chose not to do that partly because of my anxiety to mount the piece after all the years it had taken me to stitch it and partly because the edge was perilously close to tearing and I was worried the piece would become unstitched and ruined. The solution was a practical and a sensible way out (and if I had not pointed it out to you, you may not have noticed it anyway!). The second point of interest is that the guard's uniform is largely made up of a new stitch I had found that consists of alternating cross stitch over three hole squares with one over five hole squares, which produces an interesting, brocaded effect when completed. The body of the blue jacket allows the smaller of the two cross stitches to peep through in metallic thread, while the yellow sleeve enables you to make out the white canvas for contrast.

The exhibited tarts, resplendent on a silver tray, **(5)** rest on a blue cloth **(18)** worked in tent stitch in thick-gauge pearl cotton but over two canvas holes instead of one and with the stitch worked in the same way but backwards in alternate rows. This produces a different and raised texture. The undercloth **(19)** is worked in basic bargello stitch culminating in coloured hearts that are overcoated in Gobelin stitch, as is the barrister's brief on the table. The pink ribbon has been allowed to hang loose for reality.

The backdrop cloth **(6)** presented the problem of perspective for the middle ground yet again. I have attempted to solve it by permitting bits of it to stand out, while working it predominantly in tent stitch. The bulbous bits that do stand out have been worked in Gobelin stitch over an undercoat. I was pleased with the fringe, which was achieved by random slashes of stranded cotton over wool – an example of relaxation and confidence as progress is made into the piece. Not at all clever in reality, but effective for its simplicity!

At this stage I did tend to dart about doing bits of the background and the Knave **(7)**, **(3)**, **(6)** as the mood struck me. I seem also to recall working on the floor **(8)** at about the same time. As far as the background **(7)** is concerned I say simply that I set out to achieve a terracotta look (mainly because it was to be displayed in a house with terracotta surfaces, though heaven forbid that I was merely composing a decorator piece!). I wanted the surface to lack a uniform colour and to savour of the natural differences of shading that appear in this material; hence the lack of order in the shading of wall and floor tiles **(8)**. As to the terracotta floor tiles **(8)**, they were worked in a combination of pearl cotton and Persian wool in brick stitch. Notice my, by now, frequent encouragement of the canvas to show through the Persian wool!

The barristers **(9)** were a real challenge. By definition they lack colour in the sense that the other characters do not: that is to say they must remain black and white to be true to life. I have solved this in respect of the two barristers in the background by making them grey and white, thus enabling the counsel for the prosecution to predominate. The wigs make use of the fluffy stitch I have described previously, with French knots combined with Gobelin and tent stitches. The prosecutor's wig is worked in Persian wool and the remaining barristers in stranded cotton give them their own particular contrast. Having solved the problem of portraying the same shades with depth, I was confronted with a more difficult problem with the prosecutor's black gown: that is, it was quite one thing to be concerned about black, white and grey merging and appearing indistinct, it was altogether another challenge to portray black on black realistically so as to create folds without their being either inappropriately contrasted, as in a cartoon, or remaining black and indistinct throughout. I despaired for a time until one evening, while enjoying a symphony concert, I noticed that the black taffeta skirts of the cellists in the orchestra reached to the floor in folds and gave the appearance of charcoal grey on black. This was the solution; worked in thick-gauge wool in different directions for the folds and black tent stitches in the crevices.

The barristers with their black on black gowns.

I cannot pretend that I rushed home late after the concert and obtained the final result, but I could not wait to try the idea out. I think it worked. This experience underlies another important lesson for the needleworker. Do not be impatient and never make do with an unsatisfactory solution. The proper solution will present itself when you least expect it. Move on to something else until the solution appears, rather than spoil it by making do.

The guard on the right-hand side **(10)** has been removed from the Queen of Hearts' side (with appropriate apologies to Tenniel) and placed below to aid the composition and balance of my interpretation. I had a great deal of fun with this figure and had pored over the threads in the shop to pick out the precise greens that I had wanted and, in particular, the metallic threads that would lend some magic to an otherwise background character. The final result was pleasing. His helmet will not be difficult for you to analyse, but I must say that I am now glad that I did not yield to the temptation to colour the helmet entirely in metallic bronze; I really do think that the terracotta long stitch in pearl cotton enables a good contrast and yet imposes a restraint on the final result. The significant achievement otherwise is to be found in the carefully stitched Persian wool tunic in long stitch, worked in a clockwise direction over an undercoat to lend prominence to the top but done in tent or continental at the bottom, so as not to interfere with the face of the surly guard by the witness box. One must keep in mind perspective at all times!

The green sleeve is a familiar application of chain stitch over a woollen undercoat to suggest chain-mail. His white-gloved hand clutches a spike worked in pearl cotton, topped with the same copper metallic thread that is applied in long stitch to the helmet. A nice balance overall, I think.

The Queen of Hearts **(11)** was really my first attempt at depicting a human face. It is said that Tenniel had modelled this character on Queen Victoria; I kept that in mind when attempting to stitch a semblance of the Red Queen's face. Tenniel's sketch is so distinctive and canvas is a difficult medium on which to sketch, not to speak of the added problem of the minute but accumulated changes to the overall appearance made by application of the stitches (I settled for a regal look of angry impatience that captures the spirit of the story).

Her crown is worked, of course, in gold metallic thread in tent stitch at the base and topped with a long stitch application over an undercoat of gold stranded cotton, which can actually be spotted in parts and lends its own sheen. All of this is topped with the odd bead sewn on with invisible thread. The wimple is effectively worked first in charcoal grey, with the odd slash of a lighter shade to suggest sheen. Pearl earrings, invisibly stitched together with stars of the garter, mingle with a blaze of red French knots embellished here and there with a sprinkle of gold metallic thread. The Queen's bodice is worked in thick-gauge, cherry-red wool in long stitch.

Her gloved hands are done, of course, in disciplined Gobelin stitch in stranded cotton; the underside is grey since it would be shaded by the other hand. From between her ermine-edged train (worked in Persian wool) blazes her queenly, embroidered gown! Essentially it is made up of Gobelin stitch in various forms, with free-ranging, random embellishments of tacking stitches, beads and sequins (attached with invisible thread) and metallic thread. The starfish mingled with sequins for contrast are done in a spider-web stitch. The herringbone effect trimmed in blue metallic thread suggests an intermingling of her magnificent gown with the train, both tumbling onto the dais. Her lap is stitched in blocks of tent stitch in opposing directions to suggest a contrast in texture. The folds of the crinoline fall about and across her black-slippered toes and the intervals are worked in a dark stranded cotton in tent stitch giving the appropriate contrast and perspective to the gown itself, which is in Gobelin stitch in Persian and thick-gauge wool.

The dais deserves a mention. You will note that it is paler at the Queen's end. This was done on purpose. I wanted to suggest the playing of light on to a carpet. It is simply alternate rows of blue and red stranded cotton in tent stitch. The King's end of the dais is worked in the opposite direction but kept slightly darker. Overall it creates an interesting effect. I might say that it also distracts from the absence of straight lines, which, after four years of stitching, the process of stretching found impossible to overcome!

The White Rabbit **(12)** is by now a familiar figure and there is little new to say save that he presented a challenge to achieve realistic perspective to frame two such larger-than-life and highly embellished characters as the King and Queen. The unfolding scroll from which he reads the charges against the Knave repeats the terracotta colour so as not to compete, but it manages to stand out since it was worked in multiples of stranded cotton in a long stitch. A similar treatment is given to the edge of the rabbit's jerkin. Depth is achieved for both by working adjacent areas in tent stitch. His tunic is worked in long stitch in a herringbone pattern, but one lacking precision, so as to suggest a slightly crumpled look, as though he has been recently seated. The heart and the bow have been allowed to protrude over the undercoat and are in pearl cotton in Gobelin stitch.

The King **(13)** is richly embroidered in metallic thread, royal blue and purple wool and cotton, with a jewelled crown. Invisible thread was used with much enthusiasm on the Crown, but this was a delightful task that had to wait until the very end. For obvious reasons, the weight of these glittering objects would have made it difficult to keep the canvas balanced. The King's wig was kept simple: a mixture of grey thick-gauge wool in Gobelin stitch interspersed with pearl cotton in tent stitch. Peeping beneath this judicial wig can be seen his own pale grey hair worked in Gobelin stitch in pearl cotton. Between the folds of purple split satin stitch in thick-gauge wool peeps his other regalia; again a mixture of Gobelin and tent stitches as the mood struck to create a balance of red, yellow and blue. An attempt to suggest dimension has been added with the lap of blue Gobelin stitch fading to tent stitch as it gets further away. His left leg has been worked in tent stitch to allow it to blend into the background, while the right leg has been worked over in Gobelin stitch to bring it to the foreground – perspective again!

His knees are given prominence with alternating red pearl and pale blue metallic thread, with chain-stitch garters to balance the perspective of the piece. The right boot has been embellished and pronounced for the same reason. In his hands the King holds his insignia, made suitably important by multiple overcoats of gold thread.

The blue drape **(14)** has been entirely worked in pearl cotton in Gobelin stitch, which is in various directions to give contrasts and interest. I then plaited some strands of blue and gold cotton and sewed them into place with invisible thread to hold back the curtain.

The pillars **(15)** are done in the same way as previous pillars (see page 27) and they lend balance to the piece. The background **(16)** is worked in bargello patterns in stranded cotton; one pattern merges into the next so as to suggest fading of the fabric. In the course of working the piece it became a little soiled, I actually quite liked the effect since it added to its reality, so I left it.

The Coat of Arms **(17)** was worked with some gold metallic thread. I think, by now, you will be able to identify the methods employed. To give further balance to the piece I have added a suggestion of the bargello pattern **(20)** from the cloth, but in complementary shades, as though their majesties were seated against what is left of some faded Florentine back cloth. To have covered all of the background would have been too distracting – artistic licence yet again! The pale blue **(16)** could be blue sky through a window but that might be somewhat anachronistic. A back cloth is more appropriate.

A general comment should be made here about the faces. I discovered that a more realistic expression could be achieved by working a pale shade near to the main character lines, rather than a dark shade. The latter gives a more cartoon-like appearance, while the former introduces a subtlety. This can best be seen by studying both the faces of the Queen and the Knave. I purposely kept the King as Tenniel had drawn him; that is to say, a not-quite-realistic person, who has paled into insignificance beside the fury of the Queen!

ALICE AND THE QUEEN OF HEARTS IN THE GARDEN

The scene in the garden with Alice and the Queen of Hearts again owes its inspiration to the Tenniel illustration. It is an obvious companion piece to the court scene. I had begun to toy with the idea of it some years ago and had got as far as sketching it onto canvas and working some of the Queen, but had been distracted by some of the other pieces that follow. I always find it vital to have a few pieces on hand at any one time to relieve the monotony and I find it improves the final result of all of them. Variety promotes success and interest.

Its delayed completion, however, makes it my most recent finished work chronologically. The curators of the exhibition celebrating 125 years of Alice commissioned me to complete it for the exhibition. It, therefore, became my most expeditious task to date, and had to be completed in six months – which involved abandoning all else but a little sleep, some food and as conscientious a work-day as my energy would allow.

Much of the piece repeats the idiom and colours of the court scene and, as they are so similar, I shall only discuss the obvious differences and the new lessons acquired through it. A close comparison of my piece with the Tenniel original will show that I have taken a great many liberties; I hope that I may have at least maintained the spirit of the original and not in any way competed with his intention.

It is important to appreciate the exact moment in Alice's story that is represented by Tenniel's picture. The Queen has just said: 'What's going on here?' 'How should I know?' said Alice, 'It's no business of mine'. The Queen turned crimson with fury, and after glaring at her for a moment like a wild beast, began screaming: 'Off with her head!' It is therefore a moment full of sound and fury with, no doubt, a quivering Queen against a fabric of calm or fear, or both. It is that mood I set out to create in this piece.

The Queen of Hearts **(1)** is resplendent in her day gown and glitter. To suggest the extremes of rage in her face, I experimented with a white stranded cotton face with black outlines, relieved by pink fabric paint to show the aggregation of blood in the predictable areas. Her hair and wimple are worked in stranded cotton in Gobelin stitch and these are divided from her metallic-thread tiara by a row of small seed pearls sewn on invisibly. She holds a large red heart worked in Smyrna cross stitch in red stranded cotton, which was threaded on the needle together with a strand of gold metallic thread. Landing as it falls, the gold touches here and there lend lustre to a regal personage, as do the beads invisibly sewn onto the border, while the beads also lend perspective to it and bring it to the foreground away from the tiara. The

Tenniel's illustration of the Queen of Hearts interrogating Alice in the garden.

Queen's left hand is covered with a white glove with pointed cuffs worked in stranded cotton in Gobelin stitch, which forms a nice contrast to the burst of French knots on her leg-of-mutton sleeves. The sleeves are worked in wool and cotton for contrast and embellished with red beads every so often. Note the simple but effective third dimension given to the cuff on the left arm as it menaces poor Alice: the under cuff was worked simply in tent stitch, the upper cuff was worked again in Gobelin stitch in stranded cotton and divided from the hand by a pearl bracelet.

The Queen's pearl earring is sewn at an angle to capture the movement of her body (as one hopes does the cut and set of her gown generally). Her bodice is worked in tent stitch save for the sash, which is effected in loose French knots in pearl cotton centred with pale blue beads invisibly sewn into place. Of course, the right bosom is surmounted by a large crystal bead surrounded by smaller beads to suggest an order or symbolic jewel such as worn by queens. The gown is largely made up of variations of tent and Gobelin stitches in patterns familiar from previous pieces. Notable novel additions include a single spider-web starfish; a beaded lower panel on the inner fold of her red

For an explanation of the stitches used, the numbers on the diagram relate to the bold numbers in the text.

Gobelin-stitched gown; a single blue thread tied in a bow at the lower end of the blue swished part of the gown, repeating the suggestion of movement and lending perspective and dimension to the skirt. The blue and white striped effect worked in herringbone pattern interspersed with blue metallic thread seams gives an interesting complement to the line of the gown as it reaches the ground.

The King **(2)** is almost entirely worked in tent stitch to keep him in the background as he dubiously looks on and clutches his tiny heart on a stick, which is topped in stranded cotton worked in Gobelin stitch. His hat is edged in tiny seed pearls to give him some prominence and promote the middle-ground over the various courtiers at the back. Otherwise restraint abounds.

The Knave **(3)** by contrast bursts into the middle-ground as he smugly carries the King's crown **(19)** aloft on a splendid cushion. The latter has been worked in purple stranded cotton in Gobelin stitch, which is divided by a gold thread tacking stitch from the underside in tent stitch. The crown was an extravagant experience in patience, with invisible thread, beads and crystals, here I showed no restraint whatsoever! It was, of course, left until last. The ermine base and the crimson velvet centre pieces are the only suggestions of fabric; and they will, by now, be familiar in their split satin and Gobelin stitches respectively.

The Knave himself is largely worked in tent stitch to make him recede back from the Crown, the exceptions to this are as follows. His hair is pronounced in split satin stitch in a thick-gauge wool. Also, his sleeve edge is in Gobelin stitch to divide it from the cushion and lend perspective generally; while occasional yellow cotton Smyrna cross stitches appear on his sleeve and round the border of his tunic skirt to suggest quilting and add interest; the body of the tunic is worked in the now familiar herringbone effect. His right leg is given more prominence in contrast to the left one, which would be more in the background and worked in Gobelin stitch. His white-gloved hand is in stranded cotton with a Gobelin stitch overcoat – perspective again.

Alice **(4)** has, at last, a white apron, this is worked in tent stitch and edged in a loose chain stitch in pearl cotton for contrast. The mauve skirt is in stranded cotton in Gobelin stitch with random tacking stitches in black for the stripes. Her puffed sleeves are worked in rows of chain stitch. Her hair is worked in various shades of yellow through to brown stranded cotton in split satin stitch over an undercoat. The features of the face and the arms are left as mere suggestions rather than any attempt to be too clever.

The figures in the background **(5)** are actually a departure from Tenniel's original. They were stitched in various subdued hues so as not to compete with the main subjects. The purple courtier in his ermine-edged robe was allowed prominence to act as a frame for the Queen. His robe has been worked in a disciplined Gobelin stitch in stranded cotton with the various invervals in tent stitch in a darker cotton. The timid, little, green lady gives further interest to the edge of the piece, balancing the colour but fading in detail, as do the other members of the crowd, who peep out with frightened faces.

I have added a door to the cream tent stitch wall **(6)** that divides the Queen and her audience from the garden beyond. I felt this gave extra definition and perspective to the piece and invited enquiry as to what lay beyond – a perennial problem for Alice. It is not particularly notable save that I have cheated a little in that the black outlines have been ruled with a black pentel pen (upon completion of the piece, of course) and are not sewn at all. The doorknob is Gobelin stitch in stranded cotton and repeats the spherical shape of the top the gate post. To lend interest I have added some climbing geraniums **(20)** to the fence line. You will note that while these create perspective, they do tend to compete with the crown and the Knave's face, but artistic licence, together with the lustre of the jewels, make it work in reality.

The grub-stitch roses **(7)** add interest and remind the viewer that it was these that prompted the Queen's initial enquiry of Alice in the garden as to what was going on there. Only moments before, the three gardeners (who had been painting the roses red!) had instantly thrown themselves flat upon their faces in fear of the Queen's approach. Of course, the gardeners were actually playing cards. More about them later.

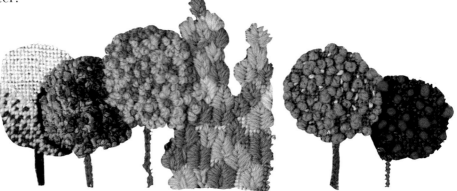

The cluster of trees **(8)** beside the glasshouse were an attempt to create a third dimension in the garden beyond the wall; keeping the effect as realistic as possible and yet allowing fantasy to creep in at the same time. The willow tree is worked in tent stitch; in front of this are ornamental trees in variations of tent stitch and French knots. Those on the fence line are in tent stitch save for the pale, central ball, which is stitched in Smyrna cross in stranded cotton. The use of black here and there adds a third dimension.

The glasshouse **(9)** was a challenge. I must admit that I unpicked my initial attempts more than once until it finally came to me that, to achieve a look of glass and metal in the sun, I could simply rely on the suggestion of metallic thread. Finally, I worked a lattice of random tacking stitches in metallic thread over a tent stitch design of large-leafed, tropical-looking greenery.

The technique for the hedge **(10)** will now be familiar – it was basically worked in Smyrna cross stitch over five squares in single strands of Persian wool. The four corners have then been diagonally stitched over in a paler colour. The distance glimpsed through the archways are self-explanatory. The background trees are slashes of cotton and wools in various shades of green, given a slight lean as if ruffled by a breeze.

The large oak or elm tree **(11)** is worked into the sky as a suggestion only and, again, given a lean. This effect is assisted by the fact that when it was finally stretched and mounted, the difficulty in getting all the straight lines true proved to be impossible. As I have said before, a problem can be turned into an asset! The poplars **(12)** are somewhat naively expressed in different shades of Persian wool in leaf stitch. There are more ornamental trees **(13)** in French knots: the largest of the three worked in wool and cotton and the one at the rear in tent stitch. Perspective creeps into this one, as the cream part is in tent stitch in stranded cotton, while the variegated green is in wool and creates its own textural prominence. The use of black again creates a dramatic outline here and there.

The sky **(14)** has been worked for a change in tent stitch. This was an attempt at creating reality tinged with fantasy, rather than total fantasy. It was also important to observe the overall perspective of the piece, so that the sky needed to fade out of the picture, so to speak, rather than achieve prominence.

The lower left-hand patch of the garden **(15)** will by now be self-explanatory. The beige and pale green flowers are further examples of the stitch I discovered by mistake referred to on page 00, when I initially worked a buttonhole stitch flower and then snipped the top with scissors. The dark green background is simply loose slashes of a slightly darker green, worked at random to add variety and texture to the bargello pattern in the background. Another patch of flowers **(16)** breaks away from Tenniel's simplicity to add some interest and dimensions to my piece. I have also added a paved path **(17)** in a bargello-type pattern to add a variety of texture and to balance the colour in the piece.

The playing cards **(18)** that are flattened in fear at the fury of the Queen, are in tent stitch in pearl cotton. Since the piece was completed to celebrate 125 years of *Alice in Wonderland*, I have taken the liberty of replacing Tenniel's depiction of the rear of the cards with the front – an ace, a two and a five. That is to say my cards have fallen on their backs rather than their fronts – justifiable licence in the circumstances!

8

MORE WHIMSY:
An Owl for a Fiftieth Birthday

*'Tis a maxim of the wise
to leave things before
things leave them.*

Baltasar Gracian

....

A good friend who turned fifty recently is a collector of owls of all shapes and sizes; so what better, I thought, than to work an embroidered owl for her collection as a special gift from me. It was also nice to be able to create a simpler, fun piece as a rest from the major and serious subjects that have preoccupied me.

I had been inspired by an idea I had seen in a magazine called *Golden Hands* to produce the piece opposite. One of the attractions of the motif was that the background canvas was basically left blank. This suited my timetable for completion of the piece. It also seemed to me that it was an excellent use of restraint in featuring the owl without any distractions. The canvas was, in fact, painted blue with acrylic fabric paint, an effect I have used frequently before and since.

The experienced eye will now be in a position to identify the stitching I employed for this piece. I am sure that you can work out for yourself the frivolous use of beads, French knots, straight slashes and chain stitch. You may recognise that the effect is achieved by Roumanian stitch on his feathers; up to this stage I did not know what this stitch was called or how to do it properly!

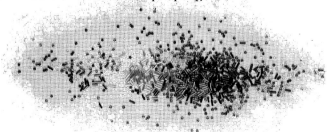

·· 9 ··

FUN WITH CUSHIONS

A good beginning makes a good ending

Proverb

· ·

In this section I feature a number of simply effected and rather unstartling cushions that have used up left-over threads and provided much needed relief from (dare I say 'cushioned') the more serious and studied projects. In most cases they have been created with a special person in mind and, for that reason, they are extremely satisfying as gifts. Certainly I enjoyed doing them and I hope the recipients have also enjoyed receiving them as much.

CHINA MOTIF

On the facing page is a photograph of a cushion that I designed inspired by an old dinner service that gives me a great deal of pleasure. The bold colours and the simple motifs of the china simply asked to be sewn! For once the entire design is worked in thick-gauge wool tent stitch and I attempted to approximate the pattern of a plate from the set. Having sketched the outline it was great fun to colour in – I could not resist complicating the centre with a mish-mash of bargello patterns fading into tent stitch in multiple strands of Persian wool. When it came to making up the cushion, Val Landman came to the rescue again.

BARGELLO CUSHION

In the photograph there is an arrangement of bargello cushions in green and lemon thick-gauge wool that I have made in a variety of patterns both for myself and others. You will notice a round cushion edged in dressing-gown cord with a miscellany of patterns. This little cushion I made for myself from scraps to contrast with the structured look of the others and as a frivolous exercise in ingenuity. The stitches and pattern employed are identified in the key below.

1 *French knots.*
2 *Buttonhole stitch.*
3 *Leaf stitch over a large number of squares, edged in tacking stitch at random.*
4 *Large, random, long-stitched circles that were roughly drawn, against a tent stitch background and interspersed with French knots.*
5 *Chain stitch intervals with slashes of long stitch in alternate directions.*
6 *Basic bargello.*
7 *Rhodes stitch worked over 5 or 7 squares.*
8 *Brick stitch.*

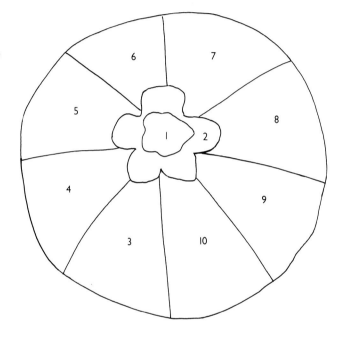

9 *Rhodes stitch worked over 3 squares.*
10 *Scottish stitch.*

STAR SIGNS

In the photographs on pages 93 and 94 are two cushions for friends who are interested in astrology. One is a simplistic depiction of the Sagittarian motif and the other a rather heraldic lion for a Leo. Both of these pieces were worked on Penelope canvas, which enabled the central motif to be worked in petit-point stranded cotton; while the surfaces are stitched in thick-gauge wool. An advantage of Penelope canvas with its double threads in this context, is that it is stronger and more durable for a chair that will get heavy wear.

The trained eye will be able to identify the former as being made up of a petit-point central motif, surrounded by thick-gauge tent stitch. covering the inset cushion of a rather basic chair acquired in a junk shop for a few dollars. It made an inexpensive but significant gift.

I carefully sketched the rather undernourished, but nevertheless elegant, centaur as close as possible to the centre of the canvas by referring to an illustration I had seen in an astrological chart. This I placed inside a circle obtained by outlining a bread plate. The eye is drawn to the centre through a frame of black and brown outlines and various appropriate random shapes in each corner. The rather sombre shades were chosen to complement the ultimate destination of the chair and to suitably reflect the dignity (albeit a little dour) of this interesting star sign. I like to think the final result is a further illustration of the effectiveness of simplicity and restraint.

The latter is again made up of a petit-point central figure **(8)** crowned in metallic thread at random and set against a background of four quadrants of scrap thick-gauge wool in bargello patterns as follows: brick stitch **(1)**, star bargello **(2)**, steps and stairs bargello **(3)** and Florentine bargello **(4)**.

The cushion was made up by my friend Val Landman in a pale green velvet and I embellished it with hand-made tassels. It now rests on a genuine Jacobean chair and adorns an elegant hall for all to see and enjoy.

For added interest and to offset my signature in the right-hand corner **(5)**, I included a fleur-de-lys **(6)** in the left-hand corner. This is echoed by the star **(7)** of the bargello pattern in the upper right quadrant, there was sufficient yellow in the lower right quadrant to leave the corner alone. Remember restraint? Altogether the cushion, I hope, achieves a sufficiently regal look to please the Leo and complement the precious and ancient chair to which it now belongs.

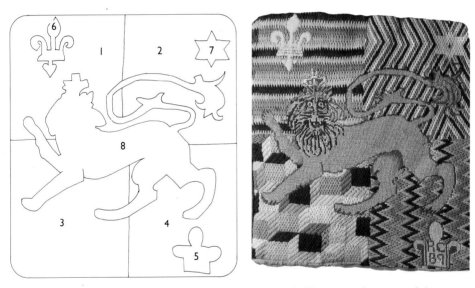

A close-up shot of the cushion showing the stitches used. For an explanation of these stitches, the numbers on the diagram relate to the bold numbers in the text.

PINCUSHIONS

The photograph on the facing page shows pincushions I have made for two good friends for significant birthdays. Coincidentally they both have names beginning with 'V', but here the similarity in the pieces ends. The little cushions were made some years apart, and both reflect my stage of development in stitching at the time. The smaller of the two was my first attempt at such a piece and what it lacks in refinement and restraint it makes up for in enthusiasm and gaiety. The background pink wool scraps and the 'V' are worked in Smyrna cross stitch, while the 'V' is bordered in tent stitch. The splash of flowers will by now be easily identifiable: it is mainly made up of French knots, buttonhole stitch and spider-web stitch. Interspersed, for added lustre, are occasional crystal beads, sewn on invisibly. The underside is a random application of multi-coloured wool worked in Rhodes stitch. The cushion is edged in pale pink braid, which is finished off in the shape of a flower and topped with a crystal bead.

The larger of the two pincushions is my most recent attempt at such a soupçon and shows somewhat more sophistication and restraint appropriate, perhaps, to my extra years and experience.

The 'V' is worked in Gobelin stitch in stranded cotton on the right-hand side and suggested in tent stitch on the left. The background is worked in tent stitch and encircled by masses of French knots, daisy slashes, buttonhole stitch, grub stitch roses and leaves all of which is set against a basic bargello stitch in green wool. The border is surrounded by braid sewn on invisibly.

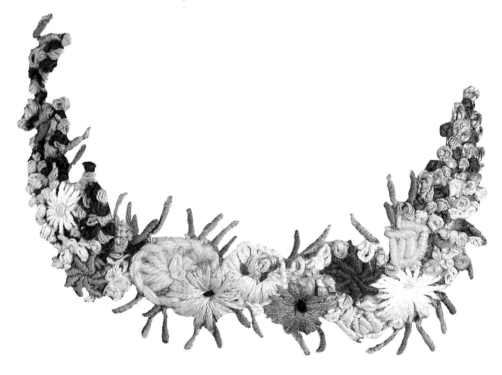

·· 10 ··

A JAPANESE LADY

Everything has its beauty but not everyone sees it

Confucius

· ·

This piece has had mixed reactions from my friends and interested onlookers. It is a fairly recent piece and is rather a startling departure from my alleged obsession with romance and chintz!

My friend Hannah Lewis has a penchant for and a great skill in designing very distinctive and bold figures. Her colours are always bright and challenging and her motifs distinct and forthright, but rivetting in their simplicity and style. I was anxious to try to colour in one of her pieces. She drew the bare outline of this Japanese lady on to a blank piece of canvas for me and I set about bringing it to life in thread and beads as a gift for some mutual friends. The stitching ideas are fairly simple and somewhat repetitive, but the design required thoughtful application and a great deal of restraint. I am not sure that I have altogether kept it restrained enough to do it justice, but by referring to the photograph opposite and the diagram on page 100, you will be able to identify the stitches and effects employed.

A particular restriction in the realisation of this piece was that the colours used were, to a degree, dictated by the friends for whom the piece was to be completed: that is to say, certain colours were to be avoided.

The hair **(1)** was worked last, and is Gobelin-stitched stranded cotton over a tent stitch undercoat. The spikes in her hair **(2)** were worked in tent stitch and topped with crystal beads to catch the light.

Hannah had drawn loose, spider-web configurations that swept in curves without too much symmetry for the top of her cloak. So, to retain the lack of formality and reflect the movement of the lines of the drawing I decided to border and work the lines **(3)** in gold metallic thread. Set against the face, neck and shoulders (worked in mustard tent stitch in stranded cotton) it hopefully gives the idea that the upper part of the cloak is transparent. Next I worked the shoulder areas **(4)** **(5)** in an attempt to suggest a padded, quilted look. The various shapes

within the web-like structure were worked in stranded cotton in Gobelin stitch in shades of the same colour, fading from dark to pale. The mauve shades then also pick up the fading idea across the bodice, which was worked flat in tent stitch, to give a third dimension to the figure.

The shades nearest the border of the cloak **(6)** were allowed to spill into the striped sweeping lines worked, yet again, in Gobelin stitch.

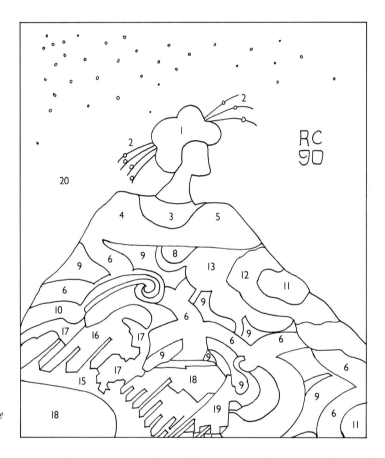

For an explanation of the stitches used, the numbers on the diagram relate to the bold numbers in the text.

You will be able to identify many other sweeping stripes of different shades; wherever possible, I have tried to select the shades to give balance to the piece as a whole. I always try to remember the artistic triangle, that is, that the same or similar colours are best balanced by repeating them in at least three separate and distinct splashes in roughly equidistant areas.

The sweeping stripe below **(7)** is given a slightly different treatment by allowing the centre to remain flat in tent stitch. The dark green is intended to balance the stamen of the flower **(11)** – the triangle at work! It is worked in Gobelin stitch in stranded cotton. The middle section **(8)** has at its centre, alternate rows of tent stitch in gold metallic thread and black stranded cotton; the border repeats the fading in idea and goes from pale mauve to dark and back to pale, dissolving into greens that then blend into the flower **(11) (12) (13)**. The background areas **(9)** represent the only shading stipulated by the artist. In various places they are worked in tent stitch and in others in French knots and Gobelin stitch to add dimension and texture.

On the left-hand side (10), stripes of tent stitch rise up from a flurry of French knots and green beads; this also to a degree fades in to the adjacent area (7).

The stamens (11) of the large green flower are worked in French knots and beads, fading from the outside edge towards the centre. The one at the bottom right-hand corner of the picture is allowed to spill out over the border. Green stranded cotton Gobelin stitch splashes fade into split-satin-stitch petals (12) that are set against a tent stitch background. The outside perimeter of the flower is treated with alternating shades of green scraps, somewhat at random, repeating the shades used at the centre. A mauve stamen (14) in split satin stitch in stranded cotton slashes fades gradually into Smyrna cross stitch lines in pearl cotton (15) and introduces straight lines – a stark contrast to all the spirals so far!

By way of complete contrast and remembering the triangle, the

 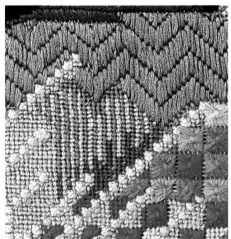

mustard shades (16) are worked into the piece in brick stitch and tent stitch to allow a variety of texture and dimension. These shades are then repeated in the spirals above (7).

At the edge (17) the tone is changed again, in the interests of texture and balance, by the introduction of mauve French knots, spider-web stitch and buttonhole flowers. A contrast of colour and pattern introduces a bargello sweep (18) that fades downwards into stripes of tent stitching.

Rhodes-stitch pink squares (19) fade into spiral sweeps, introducing a dramatic focal point to balance the overall picture.

The sky (20) was left unworked and has been painted in acrylic artist's paint, fading from left to right, and embellished with beaded stars to catch the light. The initials and year are added in an egocentric but slightly Asian gesture.

A double mount completed the effect of simplicity.

A PORTRAIT OF DAME JOAN SUTHERLAND

Even if the face is not 100 per cent
there's no doubt that it's me!
                    Dame Joan Sutherland

I saw Dame Joan recently in Switzerland . . .
and saw your needlepoint picture which looked
very accomplished.

                    Michael Stennett

· ·

My portrait of Dame Joan Sutherland is perhaps my proudest piece to date. Australians are proud of her; opera-lovers adore her; and as both, I am no exception!

Some years ago I read that Dame Joan was contemplating retirement and that she looked forward to spending more time on her garden and her needlepoint. It occurred to me that it would be a great challenge, and an exciting one, to attempt to depict her with needle and thread and if it were possible for me to capture a passable image of her then it would be a rather special retirement gift to present to her. I did and I have.

On a morning in July 1989 in Melbourne, I had the great privilege and pleasure of realising this ambition. I met my idol and handed to her a project in patience (if not in photographic precision) that had taken me more than two years to complete. The prospect of a personal meeting with the megastar was alarming, but the reality proved exciting and memorable.

The image that inspired my pièce de résistance was Michael Stennett's wonderfully romantic portrait of Dame Joan as Violetta from *La Traviata*. My choice was fitting as, in retrospect, I discovered that this is one of her favourite roles. It is certainly one of my favourite operas; and I had seen Dame Joan perform the role. It was, therefore, not difficult to find the correct mood music for my stitching sessions and, needless to say, I have had to replace my first recording with a new one!

When graciously permitting me to reproduce the photograph of his portrait that appeared on the libretto of my record set, Michael Stennett pointed out that, in fact, the actual portrait is a reverse image: that is to say the photograph that appeared on my record set had been reversed! This highlights an interesting point that I have found. One of the best ways of testing that an image is satisfactory is to hold it up to a mirror; if the reflection looks right then, assuredly, the original will be. I am not sure of the science behind such advice, but I can say that it does work. It obviously works for great artists like Michael Stennett too.

Michael Stennett's portrait of Dame Joan as Violetta in La Traviata *featured on the cover of my album. It was the inspiration for my tribute to Dame Joan.*

The diagram opposite will enable you to analyse the stitches and effects that I employed, but before doing that it is instructive to mention an early experiment, an outline sketch similar to the one from which I worked, but on thicker canvas. I abandoned this sketch finally because I needed a finer-gauge canvas to capture realism in the face.

Petit-point or etamine canvas is a must for any work with fine details; with a thicker-gauge canvas, one stitch out of place and the expression disappears altogether. I practise what I preach in this case and always retain a piece of canvas on which to try out stitches and effects, so that fear of failure does not cause me to freeze into immobility.

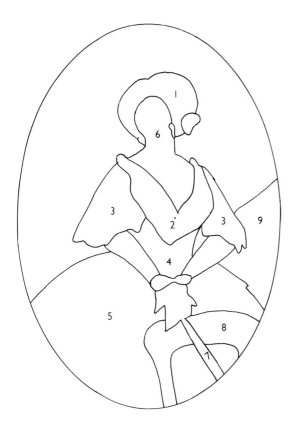

For an explanation of the stitches used, the numbers on the diagram relate to the bold numbers in the text.

A striking feature of Dame Joan's persona, on and off the stage, is her flaming titian hair **(1)**. I portrayed it in thick-gauge wool in a split satin stitch over an undercoat of tent stitch. By changing the direction of the stitches mid-temple, ever so slightly, you get the slight impression of a parting. I resisted the temptation to try to be smart with contrasting or supplemental shades of yarn in the hair and allowed the individual stitches to create their own shadows. Some simple slashes of white stranded cotton, embellished with beads and French knots, suggests an adornment in the hair.

The upper bodice of Violetta's crinoline **(2)** is worked in white Persian wool in split satin stitch that I kept short and tight, over an undercoat of tent stitch to promote the third dimension. The bodice is edged in flesh-coloured Persian wool, repeatedly applied in Gobelin stitch to create a realistic but subtle border. This border has French knots here and there that culminate on the shouders and frame another of Dame Joan's marvellous features – her décolletage.

The lacy puffed sleeves (**3**) have been worked first in flesh-coloured stranded cotton in Smyrna cross stitch to promote perspective. I then used the same technique that I applied to Alice's apron (see page 66) with chain stitch worked over the top, save that in various places and especially at the edges I have pulled loose with a needle some strands of the thread to suggest the undisciplined appearance of lace. With the occasional strand caught with invisible thread, the effect is easy to achieve. Seed pearls were then sewn with invisible thread inside most of the chains and have also been added around the edge of the sleeve, at various angles to suggest movement. It is, perhaps, not difficult to imagine that Violetta has just a moment ago turned her head and body slightly to the right!

The bodice (**4**) has been worked in stranded cotton in tent stitch in vertical rows of two stitches in one direction alternated with two rows in the opposite direction to suggest a pleated or rough textured fabric. The darker grey used for the background and to frame the bodice and waistline is done in the same way. The jewelled clasp in the centre of the piece is a crystal surrounded by seed pearls and supplemented by three vertical pearls to add interest and reality (invisible thread to the rescue yet again).

The skirt (**5**) has a thick-gauge wool undercoat and the top layer is repeated applications of white Persian wool in encroaching Gobelin stitch. This creates its own shadowed intervals in the main, without the need to resort to adding them separately with a darker thread. One or two of the intervals close to Violetta's hands have, nevertheless, been shaded in tent stitch in grey stranded cotton. From the arms outwards

I sewed small beads on the skirt, thickly at first, but gradually thinning out so that near the outer edge there are none. Knowing where to stop in this context can prove difficult!

The flesh itself **(6)** is worked in tent stitch in stranded cotton with darker shades to suggest shadows. The eyes, nose and mouth are mere suggestions that sacrifice photographic accuracy for semblance: they look better from a distance than close up. Here I resorted frequently to that practise of mine of throwing the piece onto the floor from time to time to tell whether the look from afar is right or wrong.

The jewellery generally is made up of crystals and beads applied with invisible thread. The fan **(7)** is stitched in herringbone slashes of stranded cotton.

The Victorian dining chair **(8)** was stitched with a large-eyed needle in stranded cotton supplemented with a fine gold metallic thread. Using this technique the cotton lands as it falls, so that the gold touches appear at random. It may sound a little kitsch, but the final result was not, although a true disciple of restraint might avoid this effect.

The background **(9)** was worked in tent stitch in stranded cotton to suggest a rich, theatrical, velvet backdrop. Artistic licence could then justify the extremes of shading and the black area behind Dame Joan's torso that I used to bring it into appropriate prominence. A double mount in black and terracotta frames the piece, doing it justice and lending it a third dimension.

The photograph above captures the exciting moment for me when I was able to present my portrait to Dame Joan – dreams really do come true!

POST SCRIPT:
for Hamish

The lyf so short, the craft so long
to lerne

Geoffrey Chaucer

....

I have a lovely, fat, grey moggy called Hamish and a sitting room with tartan carpet. A current project is unfinished but promises to be fun. As the photograph clearly indicates, one day Hamish will have his very own cushion, although like all cats he will probably sit everywhere else but on it!

GLOSSARY

· ·

Given that the aim of my text has been simply to inspire you to explore this creative area, and to explain my own approach to needlepoint, this glossary does not provide comprehensive details for all the possible stitches.

I have endeavoured to explain every vaguely technical term and/ or stitch that I have referred to in the text. I have done this with as much clarity as I can muster. In many cases I have included my own techniques and ideas, whether or not they concur with the approved methods of the purists or authorities on the subject. The proof of the pudding is in the eating. In any event, needlepoint is an individual art, and only learned by trial and error. What is right for me may not be right for you.

There are multitudes of texts available for those who wish to pursue the subject in more detail, or in a different way. A browse through any craft shop will satisfy both the hungry and the curious.

As far as the individual stitches are concerned, I would stress that there are a great many more in existence than I have used or described in this book.

If you wish to find more information on individual stitches or on canvas embroidery in general, I recommend the following publications, which have been of great use to me.

Question and Answer Book on Needlepoint by Sylvia Sidney. (Published by Van Nostrand Reinhold, 1974.)

Needlepoint by Sarah Windrum. (Published by Octopus Books, 1980 and later by Treasure Press, 1987.)

Country House Needlepoint by Frances Kennett and Belinda Scarlett. (Published by Conran Octopus, 1988.)

An Introduction to Embroidery by Anna Griffiths. (Published by New Burlington books, 1989.)

Zig Zag Stitching (50 New and Colourful Looks in Florentine Embroidery). (A Golden Hands Special published by Marshall Cavendish, 1972.)

Paternayan Stitch Techniques Booklet. (Published by Paternayan Bros.)

ACRYLIC PAINT Obtainable at any art supplies shop or superior stationer, this is water-soluble and dye-fast, and easily applied with a standard artist's brush. It is also referred to as 'fabric paint' and is not the same as the acrylic paint for painting houses. The brand I use is Colorpix non-toxic permanent acrylic P.V.A.

ALTERNATING CROSS STITCH See Half cross stitch.

BARGELLO This term is often equated with Florentine stitch, but it actually describes a pattern of stitches rather than a single stitch. There are multifarious patterns that fit within this description and are created by repeated symmetrical applications of long stitch in varied colours and patterns. Many of the patterns are centuries old and were worked as fabric hangings for beds or walls. Today they are popularly and effectively used for cushions. On page 90 I show as a background to a cushion of my own, three of the patterns: Gothic, Stars and stripes and Steps and stairs or 3-D boxes. The most common, and easiest pattern to work is the Zig-zag pattern. I refer to this as 'basic bargello'. The main attraction of bargello is that it is a quick and bold way to cover a surface.

See also Florentine stitch, Gothic bargello, Stars and stripes bargello, Steps and stairs bargello, Zig-zag bargello.

BLOCKING This is also referred to as 'stretching' or 'setting' and is the process of restoring the canvas, as closely as possible, to its original shape. I recommend dry-cleaning the piece first and then, depending on the extent to which the design is distorted, I either moisten it with a spray of water or soak it in a partially filled bath or basin so that the canvas becomes soft and pliable.

Armed with a good supply of drawing pins or thumb tacks and a large piece of corkboard, I then attempt to straighten the lines and bring back the design as accurately as possible to its original shape. I do not place too much emphasis on advice that suggests marking the centre of the canvas edges before one starts, or placing it on the corkboard face down. I simply remove the moist canvas from the basin, gently wring it out (as one would a precious sweater) and lay it down face up so I can observe where the distortions in the design are. I then begin gently stretching the canvas vertically and horizontally into the required shape, pinning the outer edge of the canvas alternately at the top and bottom, and on the right-hand and left-hand sides. Ensure that the pins are firm enough to secure the canvas, but loose enough to remove and replace in a different spot. With patience and plenty of pins, the desired shape will usually appear fairly quickly. Sometimes the canvas edge is frail and the threads fraying. In such a case I do not hesitate to fasten a pin in the edge of the piece itself (framing can hide a multitude of sins).

I ignore warnings about rust-free pins and the like, as any tell-tale rust will be hidden. Unless the piece is really moist to begin with the canvas may dry out during pinning and you will need to re-moisten it. I find this distracting and irritating – hence my advice to soak it well in the beginning. Too many applications of water can lead to the woollen threads becoming fluffy and will spoil the crispness of the design.

When I am satisfied that my design looks right, I put a few more pins around the edge to secure it really tightly and to avoid distortion during drying, when the piece will shrink. I stand the corkboard on thick towels on the floor and lean it against a wall in a warm, dry room (gravity will send the excess water into the towels) and ignore it for a couple of days.

As long as the picture finishes up straight, I do not worry if the outer edge is distorted. That is a detail (like the back of the piece) that no one will ever see again once it is framed or made up.

BRICK STITCH This stitch can be worked vertically, as illustrated, or horizontally. It consists of upright Gobelin stitches worked in staggered rows like bricks. It is ideal for backgrounds or where shading is needed. The first row is worked leaving a space between each stitch. The second row fills these spaces.

If you work over several threads instead of one for each stitch, it is referred to as 'double' or 'triple' brick stitch. However, I have made no such distinction and have chosen in this book to speak only of 'brick stitch' to cover all the possible variations. I leave it to your imagination.

See also Parisian stitch.

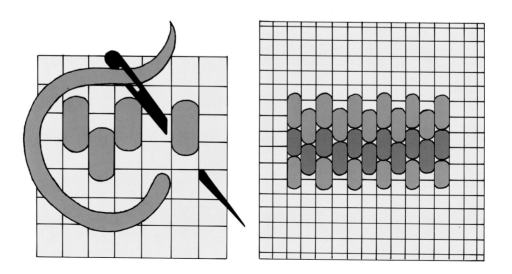

BULLION STITCH   See Grub stitch.

BUTTONHOLE STITCH   This is usually an embroidery
stitch (worked on linen in crewel thread) as opposed to a stitch for
canvas work. It is, as the name implies, also used to give a firm edge to
buttonholes. It can be worked with the stitches kept very close together
as shown in the diagram.

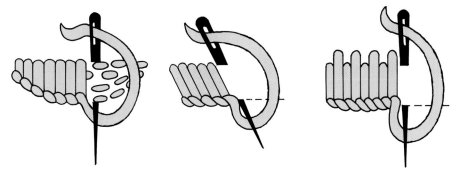

For a buttonhole-stitch
wheel, take the needle through the
same central hole, spacing the
outer stitches to suit your purpose.
If you run into problems with this
stitch, try discussing it with the
owner of a friendly needlepoint
shop, and then practice on a spare
piece of canvas to perfect it.

See also Fluffy stitch.

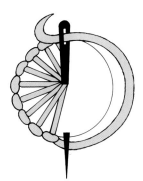

CANVAS   While there are many types of canvas available, there
are basically two types that are suitable for creative needlepoint:
Penelope or double thread canvas and Etamine or mono or single
thread canvas. The former is usually ecru or beige, while the latter is
white. Apart from the Alice in the Corridor piece, I have found it easier
and more effective to use Etamine canvas with a smaller or petit-point
gauge (18 holes to the inch). There are many others available. Your
stockist will be able to advise you, but faces and skin are obviously best
worked in the smallest possible stitches to achieve realism.

Penelope canvas has a double thread running both vertically and
horizontally. Petit-point stitching on such canvas is achieved by push-
ing each of these double threads apart so that the spaces are even (that

is to say, these areas can be worked in stitches that are half the size of those that do not push the threads apart, but cover them both). I have found from experience, however, that it is not always easy to achieve evenness of the spacing on such canvas. The obvious advantage of Etamine canvas is that the holes are small enough to allow petit-point coverage when it is required; and they are equally spaced already. When the holes are to be covered up by decorative stitching, it does not matter anyway. Etamine canvas is available in sizes from 32 to 10 holes to the inch. Penelope canvas is available from 12 to 8 holes to the inch.

CANVAS EMBROIDERY

This generally refers to any work with a needle and thread on canvas. Often called 'tapestry', though strictly this refers to woven textile work and is frequently done by machine! It is not surprising that this misnaming should occur since when needlepoint is well done it can look like tapestries. Correctly, working on a printed canvas in threads with a needle should be called 'canvas needlepoint'. Canvas embroidery is the next step, the embellishing or embroidering over the top with freehand or textured stitches. Hence my name 'creative needlepoint'. Another term used mostly in connection with embroidery on linen that is freehand and does not require counting of the threads is 'crewel embroidery'. Creative needlepoint is also often referred to as crewel embroidery; probably because of its freehand nature. It could also be referred to as 'decorative stitching'.

See also Embroidery.

CHAIN STITCH

This is used for outlining or filling.

Bring the thread up from the underside of the material at point x, hold the thread down with your left thumb and re-insert the needle at x. Take a small stitch to y and pull the needle through keeping the thread below the needle. Make the next stitch by re-inserting the needle at y. The finished effect is shown in diagram 3.

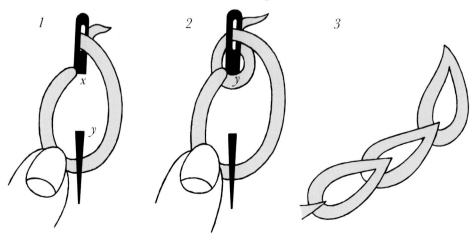

For open chain stitch, a space is left between the two threads at the top of the chain (diagram 4).

You can join the chain vertically and horizontally to create the lace look I describe in the text (diagram 5). The upper chains are left open for this effect.

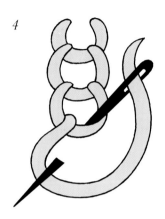

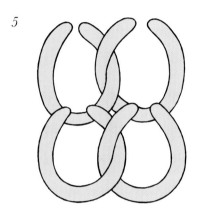

Chain stitch on canvas is identical to the embroidery stitch, and it makes an interesting knitted-look background. If worked in vertical rows, an even look is achieved by starting each row at the top. The stitch can be worked over two canvas threads on a small mesh canvas, but work each row next to the previous one on larger mesh canvas.

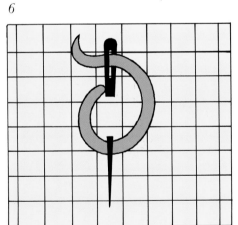

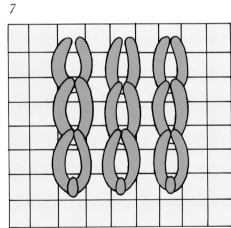

CONTINENTAL STITCH See Tent stitch; Half cross stitch; Gros-point.

CREATIVE NEEDLEPOINT See Canvas embroidery.

CREWEL EMBROIDERY See Canvas embroidery.

CROSS STITCH
The diagrams below illustrate this basic stitch on Penelope canvas.

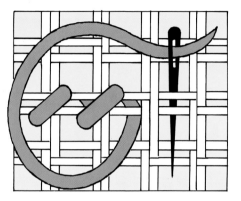 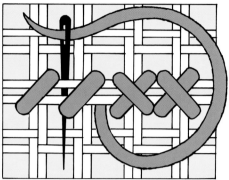

This stitch appeals to many needleworkers. Care must be taken that each stitch is crossed in the same direction. Crosses may be made separately, but in large areas it is simpler and quicker to work all the stitches in one direction first. Some pieces are worked entirely in cross stitch in preference to tent stitch, which gives them their own particular charm and effect. Worked on Etamine canvas as shown below, the pieces illustrated in this book usually have cross stitches covering three canvas holes.

See also Half cross stitch, Smyrna cross stitch.

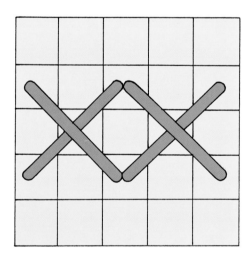

DECORATIVE STITCHING
See Canvas embroidery.

DIAMOND STITCH
Sometimes called 'Hungarian diamond stitch' as it fits in well with Hungarian stitch and is a variation of this stitch.

Work the diamonds in horizontal rows. For a solid pattern commence the next row by working the shortest stitch under the second longest stitch of the diamond above.

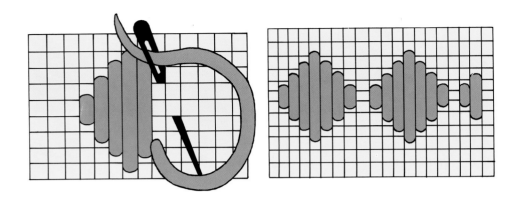

Half diamond stitch makes an attractive border or edging stitch.

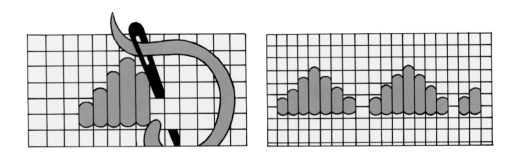

DIVIDED SATIN STITCH See under Satin stitch.

DOUBLE CROSS STITCH See Smyrna cross stitch.

EMBROIDERY A distinction is usually made between work on linen, which is freehand and generally unstructured, and work on canvas with structure and obvious holes. The former is strictly 'embroidery' while the latter is 'canvas work'.

ENCROACHING OR SLANTING GOBELIN STITCH See under Gobelin stitch.

ETAMINE CANVAS See Canvas.

FABRIC PAINT See Acrylic paint.

FLAT STITCH

This is worked over three vertical and three horizontal threads. The individual square may be worked vertically or horizontally, but diagonally is best as it avoids distortion of the canvas, particularly in large areas. To get the chequered effect, work diagonally in one direction with one colour, then turn the canvas and work the opposite diagonal in another colour.

See also Scottish stitch.

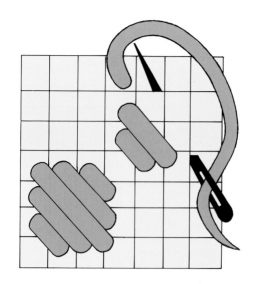

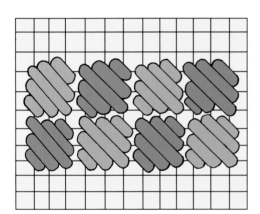

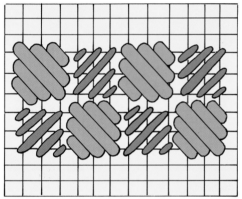

FLORENTINE STITCH

The most used stitch in bargello embroidery, this forms zig-zag and all-over wave patterns. The size of the wave may be varied by the number of stitches in each pattern and the number of canvas threads covered by each stitch. Diagram 1 below illustrates this stitch worked over four threads. Each row is usually worked in a different shade (diagram 2).

1

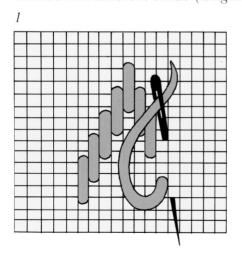

2

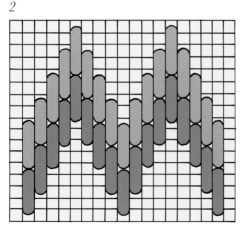

FLUFFY STITCH   Where I have referred to 'fluffy stitch' in the text, I mean a stitch that is not, in fact, a stitch! It is a flower motif that is worked in buttonhole stitch in a circle, finished off, secured at the back and then the threads are snipped through the border and the body, which causes the undisciplined teasing illustrated in the various photographs. I cannot say more, but do try it on a spare piece of canvas.

FRENCH KNOTS   This is a useful stitch and one that will be made easier by a demonstration at your friendly needlepoint shop. Once mastered it is simple, so do not be put off.

Bring the needle through the material at the spot required. Twist the thread around the needle twice and hold it tight with your thumb. Turn the needle back almost to the starting point, and push it through the material. Finish off if it is a single knot, or proceed to the next knot.

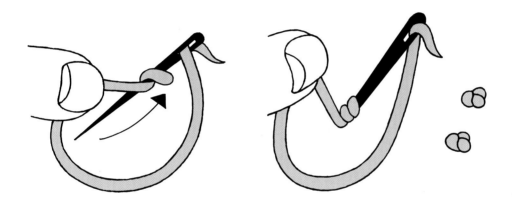

GOBELIN STITCH   This is a generic term for such stitches as long stitch, random stitch, slashes or straight stitch. According to its particular use, it is given the different names set out below. Brick stitch is yet another adaptation of it. The stitches illustrated are the traditional structured stitches.

In my text I often equate Gobelin stitch with unstructured long stitch in no particular direction or pattern. In any event, the stitches can be worked just as successfully horizontally or vertically.

ENCROACHING OR SLANTING GOBELIN STITCH   A closely packed stitch that is most suitable for shading. Rows are worked from right to left, then left to right, each stitch covering five horizontal canvas threads and one vertical thread. Each row overlaps the previous one by one horizontal thread.

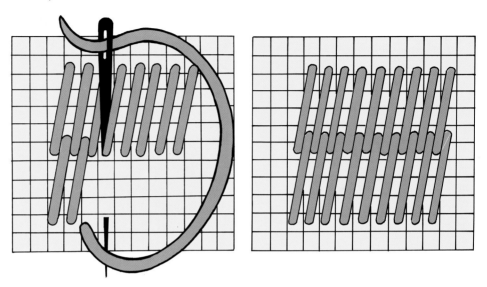

GOBELIN FILLING   A vertical stitch worked over six canvas threads with two threads between each stitch, and in rows alternating from left to right and right to left. Each row is worked between the previous one.

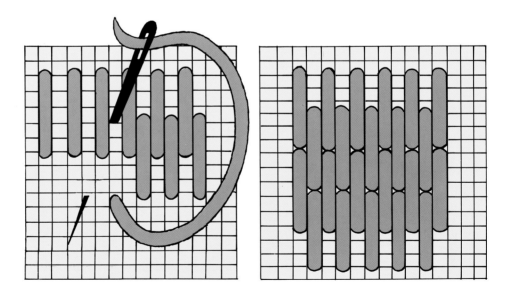

PLAITED GOBELIN STITCH   This stitch is formed by rows of diagonal straight stitches, alternately slanting to the left and to the right. The overlapping of the stitches creates the plaited effect. Each individual stitch is worked over four horizontal threads leaving the vertical threads between each stitch.

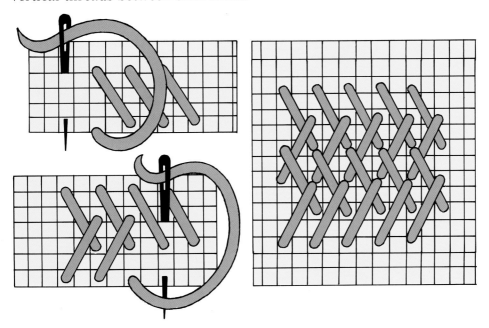

UPRIGHT OR STRAIGHT GOBELIN STITCH   This stitch can be worked in two ways.
1 As a stitch over one or more horizontal canvas threads. The illustration shows it over four threads.

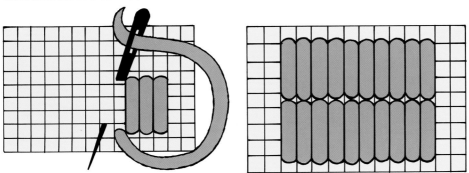

2 Where a hard-wearing or close effect is needed, a tramme thread is laid from left to right and the stitches worked over two horizontal threads.

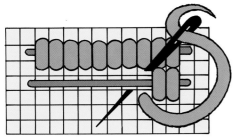 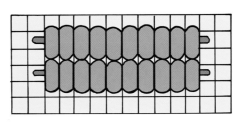

GOTHIC BARGELLO This pattern, with its curves and subtle shading, creates a flame-like effect, especially where the shading is allowed to fade slowly by clever choice of colours. The design is achieved by working the long stitch over six canvas threads, and by coming back three threads.

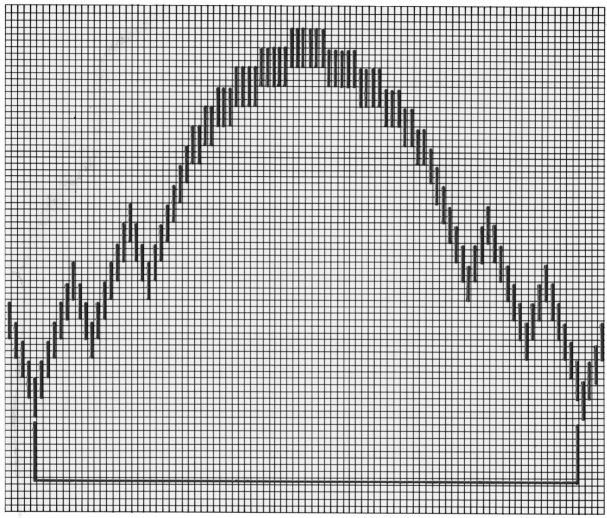

single pattern repeat

GROS-POINT STITCH This stitch resembles half cross stitch, but on the reverse side of the canvas the stitch length is greater than on the working side. This has a padding effect, making it an ideal stitch for the seats of chairs and stools.

The stitch is worked from right to left. To commence the following row, turn the canvas around and follow diagram 2.

I use the term gros-point to distinguish it from petit-point when working on Penelope canvas. In this instance gros-point means covering the double thread rather than separating them and working over an individual thread (petit-point).

1 *2*

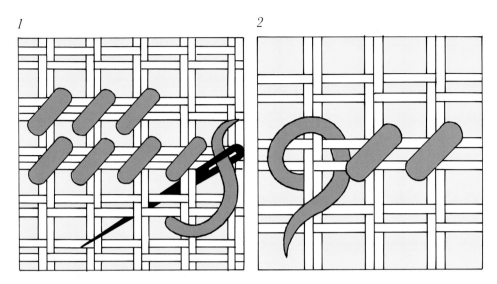

On Etamine canvas gros-point is worked in exactly the same way as tent stitch.

GRUB STITCH
This is an embroidery stitch, and it is also known as 'bullion stitch'. It is ideal for depicting wheat, barley, etc., or for roses. Use a needle with a small eye to allow the thread to pass through the coil easily.

With the thread brought up to the right side of the material, take a stitch the length required for the coil, and bring the needle back through the material at the original point (diagram 1). Before pulling the needle through, wind sufficient thread around the needle to cover the length of the stitch, hold the thread with your thumb (diagram 2), then pull the needle through.

1 *2* *3*

4

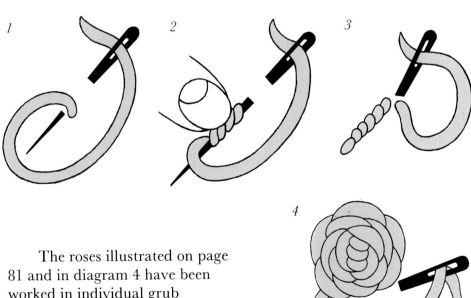

The roses illustrated on page 81 and in diagram 4 have been worked in individual grub stitches. By twisting the stitch in the desired direction, a rose-like flower is created.

HALF CROSS STITCH
This is most suitable for framed pictures and wall hangings. It resembles gros-point or tent stitch, but is worked differently. All stitches must lie in the same direction and be vertical at the back of the canvas.

There are many variations of this stitch including the oblong cross illustrated in diagram 3, which is worked vertically over five holes and horizontally over three holes. By combining this with the regular cross stitch over three canvas holes, you can create the brocaded effect I used in the *Alice in Wonderland* court scene that I call 'alternating cross stitch' (diagram 4).

1

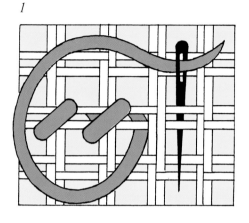

2

3

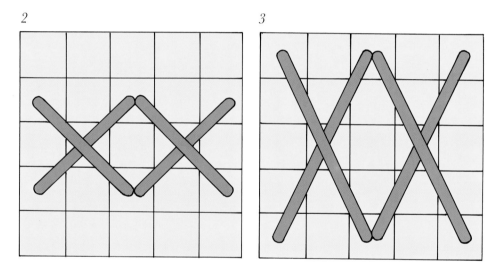

4

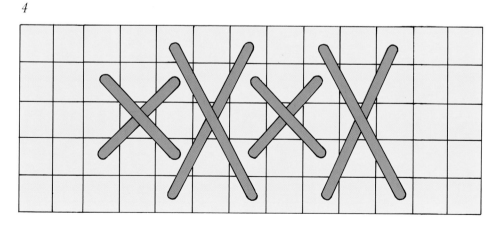

HORIZONTAL GOBELIN STITCH Gobelin stitch

worked horizontally rather than vertically.

HUNGARIAN DIAMOND STITCH See Diamond

stitch.

HUNGARIAN STITCH Hungarian stitch consists of units

of three stitches worked in horizontal rows. The first stitch is worked
over two canvas threads, the second over four and the third over two
threads. One space is left, then the next group of three stitches begins.

As a variation on this stitch, alternate rows can be worked in a
different colour (see diagram on the right, below).

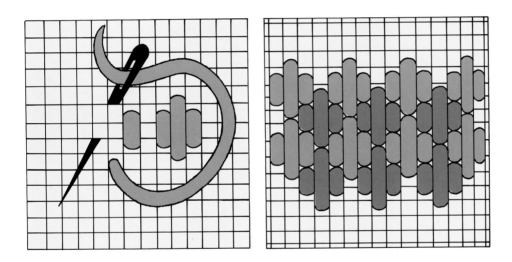

INVISIBLE THREAD This is a fine cotton or nylon thread

that comes in various neutral shades. It is actually used mostly for
sewing on beads and sequins, so that the stitches are as unobtrusive as
possible. The palest thread I have been able to find is, in fact,
impossible to see with the naked eye unless it is held against black or
some very dark shade. I find it extremely useful for holding stitches in
place invisibly (such as with the teased-out, lacy effect I describe on
page 106). It is easily obtainable at sewing thread counters, and is also
known as 'beading cotton'.

LEAF STITCH
Leaf stitch can be worked in one colour, in alternate rows of two colours or in shades of one colour grading in tone from light to dark.

Start the leaf at the top with a vertical stitch over three canvas threads (1 to 2). Continue with the stitches shown in diagram 1 (3 to 4, 5 to 6, etc.) making slanting stitches. Bring the needle out again at 3 and work the other side in the same manner.

The next leaf is begun six vertical threads from the top of the previous one. The stems are worked when all leaves are finished and may be in a contrasting colour.

LONG AND SHORT STITCH
See under Satin stitch.

LONG STITCH
See Gobelin stitch, Florentine stitch, Bargello.

NEEDLES
It is usually said that the correct needle for canvas work is one with a large eye and a blunt point. I certainly welcome a large-eyed needle as they are easy on my eyes, but as to the blunt end, I am not so sure. Obviously if one is working tent stitch, half cross stitch or whatever to effect a uniform surface, a blunt needle is essential, since splitting the thread is an unwelcome intrusion and will spoil the finished effect. However, with creative needlepoint you often need to split the yarn. Hence, I always have on hand a pincushion with many different needles (including a beading needle that is so thin and sharp it is almost invisible). My pincushion has a number of long and short blunt-ended needles, but just as many sharp-pointed ones. The idea of having multiple needles threaded with different colours and threads intended for the piece sounds organised and efficient, but I usually find that my enthusiasm to work on a piece will not allow me to waste time trying to contrive any system!

A word about threading the needle: it took me time to master the correct technique, but I assure you that if you do not already employ the method shown below, it is worth taking time out to practise it.

Wrap the end of the yarn around the needle and pull it firmly (diagram 1). Pinch the yarn tightly between thumb and finger and take away the needle (diagram 2). Squeeze the folded thread tight between the finger and thumb; press the eye of the needle on to the squeezed thread and pull the yarn through the eye of the needle (diagram 3).

1   *2*   *3*

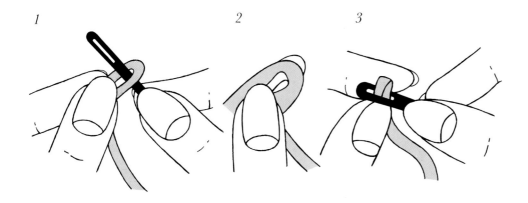

NEW STITCH   See Alternating cross stitch.

PARISIAN STITCH   This stitch can be worked vertically or horizontally, and consists of alternate long and short straight stitches. The long stitch is worked over six canvas threads and the short stitch over two threads. Each row fits into the previous one, the long stitch under a short stitch and vice versa.

See also Brick stitch.

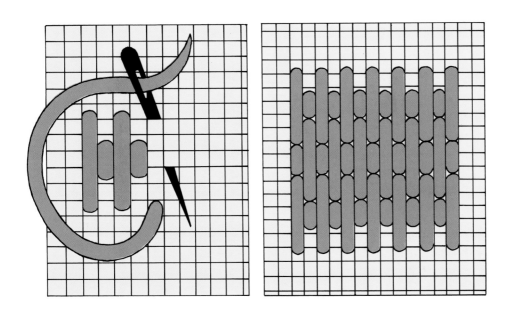

PEARL COTTON This is a twisted two-ply thread with a lustrous sheen, it is incorporated into a single thread so that it is inappropriate and impossible to divide the strands. It comes in a wide variety of colours and although I have only seen it in thick or thin gauge, it apparently is available in three sizes (size 3, 5 and 8).

PENELOPE CANVAS See Canvas.

PENTEL PENS When sketching your own designs on canvas, it is essential that dye-fast ink is used. I have found 'Pentel' pens or 'Bic' fine-line pens quite successful. If you are in any doubt, wash the canvas or dry-clean it upon finishing the sketch, but before working it. In this way if it is going to run, it will do so before you have actually stitched the canvas.

PERSIAN WOOL This is a very loosely twisted, fine, 'woolly', three-stranded wool. You can use all three strands or divide it into one or two strands depending on the thickness required and the desired effect. You can, of course, supplement it with extra threads for added thickness. It is a versatile medium, much used by me. This is the yarn that is usually supplied with canvas kits.

PETIT-POINT This is basically tent stitch worked on a fine-gauge canvas. It is used for details such as faces and hands.

On Etamine canvas work over one thread; with Penelope canvas separate the two threads and work over one thread only.

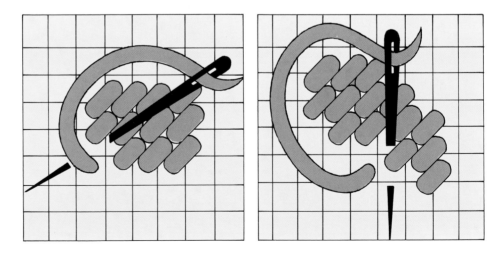

PLAITED GOBELIN STITCH See under Gobelin stitch.

POM-POM STITCH
This stitch is formed by repeated applications of a very loose tent stitch worked close together on the canvas. Each stitch should be caught underneath as it is made so that the thread does not pull through. It is best if given a thick application and each new stitch splits the previous stitches (a sharp needle should be used).

RANDOM STITCH
See Gobelin stitch.

RHODES STITCH
This is a raised filling stitch worked in a square of six vertical and six horizontal canvas threads.

Bring the needle up at 1 and make a diagonal straight stitch to 2. Continue around the square until it is filled in. Finally a small vertical straight stitch is worked in the centre to tie down the threads.

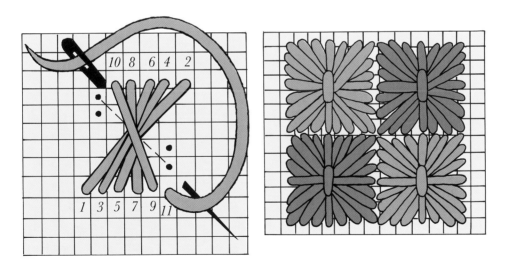

ROUMANIAN STITCH
A version of satin stitch that is very effective for leaves, etc.

Bring the needle up through the material at the top left-hand corner of the space to be filled (x) and insert it at the top right-hand side (y). Bring it up again at the centre point with the thread below the needle. Catch the horizontal thread by inserting the needle below the last thread. Then bring up the needle on the outline and repeat the process.

These two stitches are repeated until the space is filled. The centre crossing may be varied by making it longer, sloping it or making straight small stitches.

Keep the edge even to give a good result.

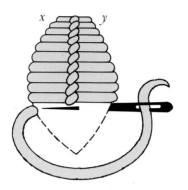

RUNNING STITCH See Tacking stitch.

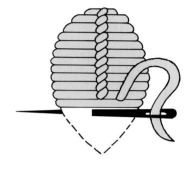

SATIN STITCH (1)
This stitch is suitable for working circles, leaves, petals, etc. Do not make the stitches too long. If you want a more padded effect, first pad the area with tent stitch. Work the satin stitch evenly and close together in the opposite direction to the padding, keeping an even edge. Keep the thread to the right of the needle.

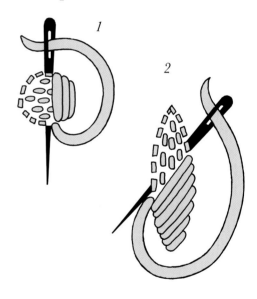

SLOPED SATIN STITCH (2)
With this the satin stitch is at an angle.

DIVIDED SATIN STITCH (3)
Use this where the area to be worked is too wide for sloped satin stitch. Mark a centre line and work two rows sloping in opposite directions.

See also Split satin stitch and Long and short satin stitch.

SCOTTISH STITCH

This is a version of flat stitch, outlined with tent stitch. It may be worked in either one or two colours. Working the tent stitch diagonally helps prevent canvas distortion. The flat stitch then fills the squares.

See also Flat stitch.

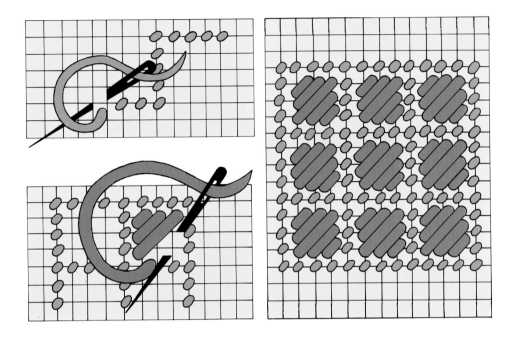

SETTING   See Blocking.

SHEAF STITCH

This is a quickly worked stitch used for filling large areas.

Bring the thread from under the canvas and work three vertical straight stitches (diagram 1). Tie these across the middle with a small horizontal stitch (diagram 2); this may be in a different colour. If you prefer, you can use two stitches across the middle.

This stitch can be worked as a continuous line (diagram 4).

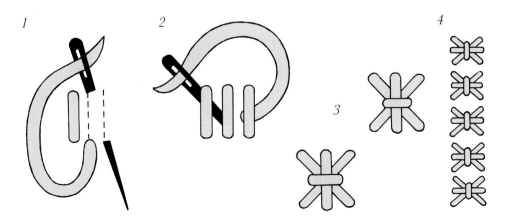

SLANTING GOBELIN STITCH See under Gobelin stitch.

SLASHES See Gobelin stitch.

SLOPED SATIN STITCH See under Satin stitch.

SMYRNA CROSS STITCH Also called 'double cross stitch', this can be worked over four threads vertically and horizontally or over two threads (the illustration shows four threads).

Begin by working a cross stitch. Then over that work a vertical cross. To keep a uniform appearance make sure the last stitches of the vertical crosses lie in the same direction.

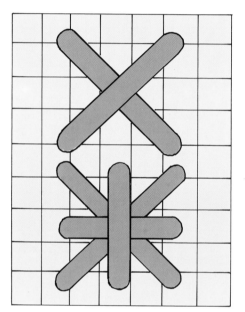

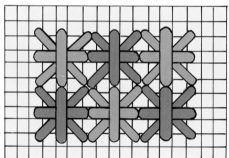

SPIDER WEB This stitch gives an interesting textured effect.

Using a tapestry needle, bring the thread through at point 1, re-insert at 2. Work in the same way following the sequence of numbers shown in the diagrams. (Note that 8 is closer to 4 than 2.)

Bring the needle out at 9 and run it under all the strands at the centre; loop the yarn over the needle and pull it through to form a knot.

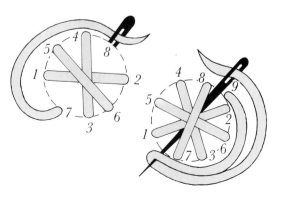

Working clockwise, run the needle under two strands at the centre, then under the last strand again and one new one. Repeat this, going back over one strand, forward under two, until the spokes are filled to the required amount.

If you want a woven spider web rather than a whipped one, work as already described until the spokes have been knotted at the centre, then, working clockwise, weave under and over the spokes until all are filled.

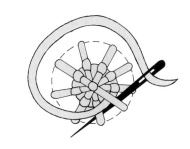

LONG AND SHORT SATIN STITCH   A stitch used for outlining or filling in areas.

Start on the left side with a small running stitch and work around the outline ending on the right side.

Commence the long and short stitches with a sloping stitch and continue alternating the stitches, keeping them close together and retaining the slope. The thread should always be to the right of the needle and the stitches must slope down to the inside centre (diagram 1).

To add further rows, take stitches up to or just between those of the row above (diagram 2).

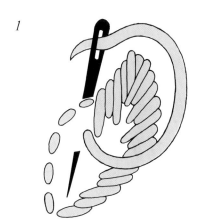

1

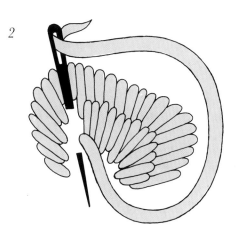

2

SPLIT SATIN STITCH   As the name suggests, this is a form of satin stitch, but the second row of stitches splits the first row, and so on. A sharp-pointed needle is required for this stitch. Application may be random or structured depending on the effect you want to achieve.

SPLIT STITCH   Commence with a back stitch as shown below. The stitches should be small and even. When taking the second stitch, insert the needle through the preceding stitch instead of in front of it.

You can make the stitches very long for extended back stitch.

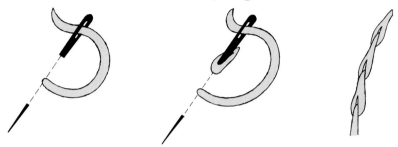

STARS AND STRIPES BARGELLO   This is a design that radiates from a central star. Each long stitch is worked over four canvas threads, coming back two threads. A lot of counting is involved at first, but patience promotes success, and once the first three stars are in place, it is easier to place the rest.

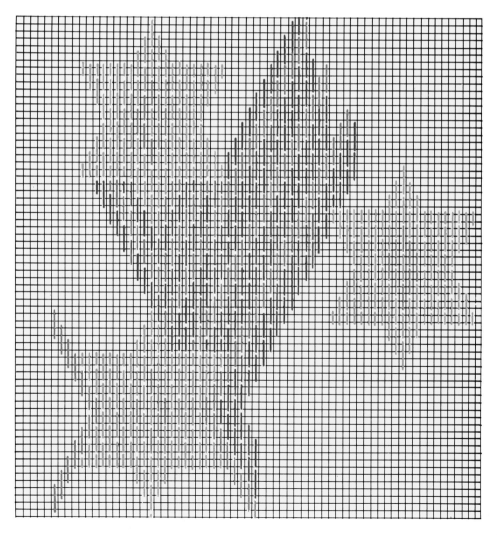

STEPS AND STAIRS BARGELLO

This is a design where each box is worked in three separate shades or colours to give a three-dimensional effect. Work forwards over four threads and back three. Where the three colours meet, four stitches will enter the same canvas hole.

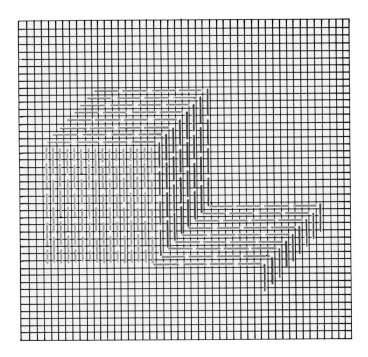

STRANDED COTTON

This is a basic thread that I use a great deal, it is available at all craft stores. A good, all-purpose, strong, fine thread, it comes in an extensive range of colours and has a slight sheen to it. It is usually made up of six separate strands of cotton loosely twisted together. The individual strands can be separated out so that for petit-point faces and skin, for example, three or four strands may be used, while on a larger gauge canvas nine strands are sometimes required for good coverage. It is a matter of choice – and trial and error. Conventional canvases take on an especially fine look done in this medium, largely due to its natural sheen.

A drawback for the inexperienced is the tendency for the individual threads to work loose and spoil the textural tightness. Tangling can also be a problem. It is very important when using this cotton to use only a fairly short length and to uncurl it every so often. This will help to give proper flat coverage.

STRAIGHT STITCH   See Gobelin stitch.

STRETCHING   See Blocking.

TACKING STITCH

This stitch is also called 'running stitch' or 'dressmakers' tacking stitch'. The thread is threaded in and out of the material along the line to be worked, keeping the stitches to an even length.

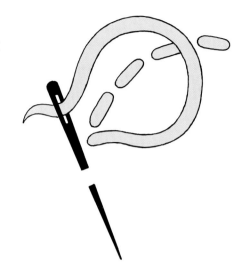

OVERCAST TACKING STITCH
Work the running stitch in the usual way then, using a contrasting thread, whip over each running stitch going through the stitches and not through the fabric, to make a continuous line.

TENT STITCH
Competing books give very complicated and confusing explanations of this very basic stitch, and variations on it, mainly by reference to the differences in how the back of the canvas looks! Actually the purpose of the references is to explain how the stitch will cover the canvas. Essentially, however, all variations are basically the same stitch.

The illustration shows how I work what I call 'tent stitch'. I accept that half cross stitch looks the same on the front, but it is different on the back as it only covers the holes of the canvas, leaving the threads visible between the stitches.

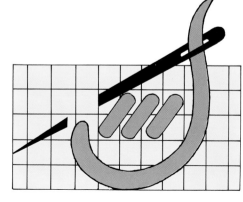

Tent stitch is also called 'gros-point' (as opposed to petit-point). I think this is a misleading name, as the latter is achieved by exactly the same method although it is a smaller stitch. Gros-point is worked the same way as tent stitch, but over the double threads of Penelope canvas.

The main thing to remember when working this stitch is to ensure that the direction of the stitch is uniform. This necessitates turning the canvas around for each alternate row unless you are starting again at the beginning. There are stitching orders that are suggested to avoid canvas distortion, but I find this stitch easier, and as effective as any for good results.

THICK-GAUGE WOOL
This is a term I use to distinguish what is often referred to as 'tapestry wool' from Persian wool. It is the most common thread recommended for use on conventional canvases. It is the coloured yarn one sees in abundance in craft shops and consists of a tightly twisted, four-ply wool. It can be used singly on coarse canvas to give a neat effect in creative canvas work.

THREAD
See Invisible thread, Pearl cotton, Persian wool, Stranded cotton, Thick-gauge wool.

TOPCOAT
This is my term for any creative stitch that is worked over the top of an undercoat of tent or long stitch.

UNDERCOAT
See Topcoat.

UPRIGHT OR STRAIGHT GOBELIN STITCH
See under Gobelin stitch.

ZIG-ZAG BARGELLO
A simple bargello stitch, also known as 'Florentine stitch'. It is worked forward over four canvas threads and back for two threads. The illustration shows a zig-zag pattern of ten stitches.

Different effects can be achieved by using either the same colour, subtle shades of the same colour or totally contrasting colours. Do use a blank piece of canvas to experiment – it is fun.

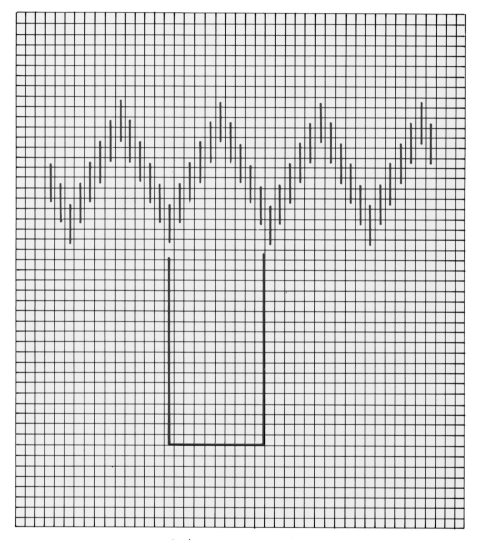

single pattern repeat

ACKNOWLEDGMENTS

....

The author would like to acknowledge the co-operation, support and enthusiasm for this project – both for various individual items and for the total concept – from the following people and organisations.

For kind and gracious permission in respect of copyright generally and, in particular, their very generous tributes to my work: Dame Joan Sutherland and Michael Stennett. Special thanks must be recorded to Dame Joan for her patience, assistance and encouragement – a great lady indeed.

For practical solutions, assistance and co-operation, and permission to use copyright material: Richard Bonynge; Moffatt Oxenbould; Stephen Broadhurst; Heather Grant and Josephine Ridge of the Australian Opera Centre: Ken Mackenzie-Forbes; Megan Dawes of The Moving Words company; Brigitte Ickmans of Imps, Avenue Louise, 391, 7B1050 Bruxelles on behalf of Pierre Culliford (the creator of Smurfs); Lockwood Tower Pty Ltd on behalf of Felix the Cat Productions Inc. trademarks; the MacDonald Group on behalf of Noddy Enterprises; Hodder and Stoughton, publishers; Dover Publications Inc., New York, and Constable and Company Limited, London, for the images from the *Alice in Wonderland Colouring Book*; McCall's Needlework and Crafts; Priscilla's Tapestry of 1205 High Street Armadale, Victoria; Hannah Lewis; Coats-Semco of 89 Peters Avenue, Mulgrave, Victoria for allowing me to use the explanations and diagrams in the book *One Hundred Stitches for Embroidery, Tapestry and Canvas Work* published by Coats-Semco and for the help given by John Betts, the Company Secretary of Coats-Semco; and Rodney De Boos.

For their stimulation, loyalty; support, promotion and encouragement: Beverley and Patrick McNally of Bargello, 819 Glenferrie Road, Hawthorn, Victoria; Priscilla, Jan and Bette of Priscilla's, 1205 High Street, Armadale, Victoria; Handcraft House, 200 Glenferrie Road, Malvern, Victoria; Myer Melbourne Craft Section, 1st Floor, Lonsdale Street, Melbourne, Victoria; Val Landman; Peter Steer; Yolanta Novak and Evan Green of Radio 3AW, Melbourne; Jacinta LePlastrier of the *Age* 'Good Weekend'; Judy Ostergaard of *Sun News Pictorial*; Mary Lou Gelbart of ABC Radio National; John and Kerry Paull of the Carroll Foundation; Jack Salter; Carole Bartlett and Rebecca Borden.

For dedication in helping me to meet deadlines and to cope with moments of despair and self-doubt: Verian Sorensen, Charles Henshawe, Helen Vimpani, Stella Folie, and my mother, Marjorie Capes.

For lending me their possessions: Marjorie Capes, Helen Vimpani, June Whiting, Sue Corke, Verian Sorensen and Val Kinchin.

For photography and artistic input generally: Stephen Broadhurst and Stephen Moreland.

For the flowers that decorate the photographs: Kevin O'Neill of South Yarra.

For generous assistance with props for the photographs: Peter Hyde, Jim Wootton, Ruth Guthridge and John Watson.

Last, but not least, I must record my gratitude and admiration for the tireless enthusiasm and consummate artistry of Theresa Janssen as editor, Karen Trump as designer and John Brash as photographer, all of whom combined their talents to make this book happen.